Scone by Scone

Tales from an Innkeeper's Life

Deedie Runkel

For Megan
Enjoy your stay.
♡ Deedie

CONTENTS

DAVID RUNKEL

Loving helpmate. Creative Chef. Cheerful host.
Chancellor of the Exchequer.
Unwavering vision.
Tireless.
A thoroughly decent good human.

This book is dedicated to you.

Ashland, Oregon
February 2018

FOREWORD

Our parents were members of the gold watch generation. Their example growing up was meant to teach us that no matter how frustrating the job or enticing the offer from another company, you were in your job for life. Having come of age in the Depression, they were determined not to take any chances.

So they were quite surprised when my husband and I did – over and over again. We moved from one city to another as journalist David was promoted from small towns to the state level to the White House. I quit a really good job because I was sexually harassed (not that we called it that in those days), and another because I couldn't stand its tedium anymore. Later, the closure of the *Phildelphia Bulletin* gave David some time off he hadn't anticipated.

Our career history relates to the stories you're about to read because it formed our personal prologue for the rest of our life. We may have been financially strapped from time to time, but somehow, despite what our parents said, we always had confidence that someone or something good would come along.

That is, until 2001. We were unemployed, 60, and out of confidence. Out of that sorry state came a transcontinental journey, and the resulting realization that we could do something else entirely.

When David's mom came to visit after our return, she was incredulous when we told her our plans. "This could never have happened in our time," she said.

And that was just the beginning. Reinventing ourselves as our own bosses 3,000 miles away from where we started turned out to be the best job we've ever had. And the longest-running. And made us the happiest hosts you could ever have imagined. Over 15 years of innkeeping, many guests have been transformed into friends, a richer bounty than we could ever have hoped for.

In the pages ahead you'll meet them and see how it happened.

Many stories collide here -- we could all write a book. Thank you for welcoming us so graciously into your story. We look forward to writing ourselves into it again in the pages to come.

— Susanna's room, 5/22/05

The Importance of Wiggling

Once there was a girl, hips quite thin,
Who stayed for a time at an Inn.
The breakfasts were vast,
And alas, soon her ass.
Twas a shame, but she'd go there again.
John, 10/10

"**A** pubic hair in the bathtub, or anywhere else, for that matter, is an absolute deal breaker."

This was maybe the eighth year of our innkeeping career and my spiel at the first staff meeting flowed as freely as the hot water from the tea machine. I'd grown to love the shock on their faces when they heard what kind of hair I was most concerned about. Attached to their meeting agendas was a photo of "The Dreaded Guest." She had hair down to her ankles. But now they were really shocked.

"We also don't want our guests worrying about a cobweb hanging down from the ceiling or a dust bunny they found under their bed *or* whose underwear they found in their drawer – better to be concerned about where they're going for dinner!

"Finally, before you leave the room, you look around and ask yourself, 'Would I pay almost $200 a night to stay here?'" Everyone always gasps a little when they hear how much it costs to stay at Anne Hathaway's. I always hear someone say, "I could never afford *that!*"

And I think they're always surprised when I tell them the truth about us -- we can't and don't spend that amount of money on lodging either.

When I'm done with my presentation, I go around the room and ask each person to share with the others what they do for fun. "Having fun is an important part of working here," I say. "You'll find the guests interesting and they'll be interested in you. Not all days are going to be full of fun, but we do encourage it."

Lindsay, a tall, tan and handsome young man who looked like he just came off the beach with his surf board spoke up first. " I just like to laugh," he said, smiling. That made us all laugh.

"I'm really into environmental stuff so working here is cool because the Runkels are too," Vieve, back for her third year said.

This was our first year with a manager. Alissa had been part of the crew for four years and had assumed more and more responsibility, including this year's staff recruiting. "Hey, guys. I'm the one to come to when you have a problem and I'll come to you when I have a problem with you. We talk a lot around here. 'Keeps the issue-level down. What I do for fun is garden and brew gluten-free beer." Everyone clapped, and with that, another season was underway.

No matter how hard we work to bring together a top crew, early spring finds me watching warily as each morning's routine gets underway. This particular day had a rough start. The weather was so chilly and threatening that we couldn't eat outside. There were so many people for breakfast, we had to add another table to Granny's table that seats fifteen. The very long tablecloth we usually use for this configuration was nowhere to be found and the few big ones someone pulled out of the closet that's supposed to look like department store stacks had more wrinkles than my face, Eleanor Roosevelt and Grandma Moses' put together.

Erin and Lindsay had never worked breakfast before, so didn't know the drill at all. And it was David's day off, which meant I was doing nearly all the cooking. Alissa's assignments were doing the fruit plates, cooking the meat, squeezing the orange juice and training our new staff. We both kept getting interrupted. Nearly every guest who came into the dining room as we feverishly put together the tables wanted something different.

"Decaf coffee? We'll have it out in five minutes. Sure."

"You'd like almond milk with your tea, that's no problem." Alissa disappeared to get it.

"Oh yes, we do have lemons for your tea. So sorry we forgot this morning. Yes, I know it's your last morning. Did you enjoy *Romeo and Juliet* last night?" I ask, shoving the fifth and final leaf into place and whispering to the returning Alissa that now we needed lemon.

While Alissa and Erin wrestled the extra table into place, I quickly wrote out the day's menu on the ancient chalkboard we use to tantalize guests with what's coming for breakfast

> Ginger scones
>
> Fabulous Fruit
>
> Aunt Til's Golden Cheese Puff
>
> Frizzled Ham

Aunt Til's is a mainstay, but sometimes a little tricky. You want it to wiggle, "but not too much," my mother's sister had instructed us. For this big a pan this getting the wiggle level correct was going to be a bit of a challenge. I worried as I wrote while Aunt Til baked away at 350 degrees. *Maybe I should have chosen something easier!*

I was also worried in my capacity as Social Director. This big group we'd had for the last few days hadn't really bonded yet. The evidence of this was long silences, stilted conversations and dog tales (the default topic *always*). It included a foursome of retired professors who come every year; a family looking at Southern Oregon University for their daughter; a slightly well-known clarinetist here to play for the Symphony (for which we provide free accommodations as a way of contributing); four women who love to come to Ashland to shop and see whatever comedies are playing at the Festival; a British couple who'd been with us all week and constantly provided not always positive comparisons of Ashland with the "real" theatre in London and the *real* Anne Hathaway's; and a Zumba instructor and her husband from Humboldt County, California. The latter had just arrived.

"Can you think of a good garnish for Aunt Til?" I asked Alissa from my scone perch.

"I'll find one," she said.

As I beat the dough down, Zumba popped into my mind. I'd only vaguely heard of Zumba once while waiting in line at an airport. The woman ahead of me was practicing new moves with her Ipod playing full blast. But when our current guest Marla made her reservation, I learned more. She said she's done all sorts of things in her life, but now that she's into Zumba, that's all she does.

"Google it," she said.

I did. Here's what it said:

Are you ready to party yourself into shape? That's exactly what the Zumba® program is all about. It's an exhilarating, effective, easy-to-follow, Latin-inspired, calorie-burning dance that's moving millions of people toward joy and health.

Hmm. Then I remembered Marla's last name – Joy! No wonder Zumba was right for her. Remembering this, I couldn't imagine how our current guests would react to hearing about Marla's job. This particular morning promised to be daunting because of the weather – other mornings people were eager to get out for a good spring walk so they didn't linger long over breakfast.

Finished with the menu, I returned to the kitchen to check on Aunt Til and the scones, each cooking in a different oven. Alissa stayed behind to show Lindsay and Erin how to set the table. I took the scones out and turned Aunt Til up a bit – she was still runny, nowhere near a wiggle.

"We're going to need a centerpiece, Miss Deedie. This table is entirely too plain and bare," Alissa said as returned from the dining room. "Do we have some flowers to pick?"

"We don't have any, but I noticed that empty house down the street has some beautiful roses. I'll go get them if you put the scones and jam out for the guests, start the meat and keep an eye on Til. Are our 'newbies' doing okay?"

"Really well. They even know which side the fork goes on. Go ahead. We're in good shape."

I took the clippers and ran down the street to the house that competes with us for short-term stays, a VRBO[1]. Because they undercut us in price, don't pay any taxes, or bother to get the permits we have to, I've decided that borrowing a few roses occasionally when it's not occupied is okay. Besides, the bumper rose crop was the perfect color for the day's table. I tiptoed to reach the really full blooms and carefully placed them in my basket. Once done, I jogged back up the street and into rear of the kitchen. As only a former florist's employee could, I had those roses arranged in a crystal vase my mother got for a wedding present within minutes. Despite all the morning's challenges, things were turning out well. *Why had I worried so?*

Placing the rose arrangement in the middle of the table, I encountered the Brits. "Now which rose is that? I don't remember seeing it in your garden," Bea inquired.

"Oh, I don't know the name of it, sorry. It's actually one of my neighbor's," I tell her, feeling a tad guilty.

"And can you tell us more about Aunt Til?" her husband asks, peering at the menu blackboard.

---

[1]   Vacation Rental by Owner

"The food or the person?" I ask back, trying to head to the kitchen to see if how Aunt Til is coming along.

"Oh, we can wait. I just thought maybe she was someone all Americans knew about and because we're foreigners, we were in the dark," he said, smiling for one of the first times in three days.

"Oh, she really is my aunt," I say, opening the door to the kitchen. "I must go check on her now."

By now, Alissa, Lindsay and Erin were lining up the fruit plates, preparing to fill them with pears we'd poached the night before.

"These look luscious," Lindsay said. "I could eat one right now. This is going to be a great job, I can tell."

"But no eating the pears until we have leftovers," Alissa counseled. "All leftover eating is confined to after the guests are served, okay?"

"Come look at this," I asked Alissa as I opened the oven to inspect Aunt Til. "What do you think?" Since Alissa's the only one of us who's actually been to Culinary School, I always consult her when I'm nervous.

"She's going to be fine. Remember, we want her to wiggle just a little bit. Whoops, the birds are singing. Time to serve," Alissa moved back to the fruit preparation zone. The Audubon Society clock on the wall provides our daily signal that it's time to serve, when the Baltimore Oriole begins to sing at 9 a.m.

I closed the oven, picked up two pear plates and moved to the dining room. People were beginning to gather. I took one last look at the table and reveled in its singular beauty. It was truly picture perfect; the roses looked as if they'd been dyed to match the tablecloth.

"C'mon, Breakfast Clubbers. Find yourselves a seat," I called to the crowd of guests milling in the living room.

Like school children lining up outside the classroom, they obediently filed into the dining room and began to take their seats. They were so quiet I felt like telling them we were all going to sing a song now or something.

"Good morning, sunshine," Marla said. She and her husband were the last to enter, a burst of energy in the midst of some near-dead batteries.

"Here she is," I said. "Our Zumba expert. Hey, Marla, introduce yourself and Sam to everyone while I go check on our breakfast."

Another fifteen minutes on the bird clock and the staff and I marched forth from the kitchen with Aunt Til quivering on every plate next to lovely sliced avocadoes artfully arranged on a piece of red chard. I introduced my Arizona aunt as a role model for all things domestic, for whose influence I was thankful on a daily basis.

"This is certainly an interesting way to meet your family," Bea said. "Aunt Til looks quite delicious."

"I know she is, because I've had her before," Marla said. "So cheesy and perfect. Now, I have to ask, did everyone like "The Coconuts" last night?"

I returned to the dining room just as a lukewarm conversation about the Marx Brothers show at the Festival was cooling off. I already knew it was near the bottom of most of our current guests' lists, having been deemed "silly." I did not reveal that I'd already seen it twice and planned to return. By the time I'd finished pouring coffee, and after a few silences, I asked Marla Joy to tell us more about being a Zumba instructor at her local senior center.

People seemed interested, if not a little taken aback. A precious few knew what Zumba was.

One older woman named Pearl said, "I just could never get my body around all those moves it has. I've seen it on TV and it looks hard."

"Getting the moves right isn't the point of it," Marla reassured her. "The point of it is to have fun! Enjoy that music. Experience your body! You'll like it." Her enthusiasm was as contagious as chocolate with a good red wine.

"Where can we go to experience it?" Les, a balding gentleman in a bright green golf shirt who had been non-participatory up to then asked. "Is it not somewhat *Hispanic*?"

One of the professors, burly in a red flannel shirt, looked at his watch and nudged his wife.

"We could do it right here, if you're really interested. 'Chair Zumba' is great for beginners. Do you really want to try?" Marla jumped up and looked around the room expectantly.

There was immediate group consensus, albeit a little nervous. The man in the red flannel shirt bolted, but his wife remained. Marla's husband, Sam, said he had just the right sound equipment for this size group. He reappeared seconds later to get the necessary set-up.

I worried that the Very Serious Shakespeare types might find Zumba a little out-of-character. I also worried what kind of stress Zumba might have on our century-old chairs. But the atmospherics in the room were suddenly lighter. Guests were up, pushing those antique chairs back, tentative but eager. Marla kicked off her Birkenstocks and threw back her long wavy salt and pepper hair.

I asked the Brits if they'd heard of Zumba. They hadn't.

"I don't imagine that's the kind of thing we'd ever hear about," Bea said. "Really."

"You'd be surprised," Marla said, "It's spreading all over the world. Do you have a senior center near you?"

Bea shook her head. The shake had some disbelief rolled into it.

The mother of the prospective college student was enthusiastic. "Oh, I'm sure you're going to like it," she said. "It's very easy to learn and the music's great! I go to a class at the Community Center twice a week."

Other new members of our housekeeping crew -- Emma and Danielle -- arrived and, as if they did it every day, pulled up chairs just as the music started. While the guests were eating, the staff had fanned out to make beds and tidy all the rooms.

Somehow it all looked enormously normal -- seventeen guests and our workers in their maroon aprons intent on following the lead of our guest whose last name was Joy.

A combination of mambo, samba and flamenco, the music made you move whether you wanted to or not, as infectious as the common cold. As I stood there surveying the situation, I couldn't stop grinning, or moving. The morning had certainly required more than the usual number of worries and contortions, but all had turned out well. The staff was even getting a lesson in how to be flexible with guests, body and soul both. Relieved, I sat down and started trying to follow the Colombian music now blaring from the tiny speakers Sam had set up. Marla's moves came fast.

Her loose clothing in deep, rich colors made it easy for her to move her hands up, down, sideways and then all around. Once I saw the muscles in her forearms and upper arms, I believed everything she and others had said about how good Zumba was for keeping muscles toned.

Sitting between two of her colleagues, Emma embodied joy, somehow picking up all the moves instantaneously. One spontaneous "Ole!" after another popped out of her mouth, one arm going down, the other up. I ducked into the kitchen to get a stool so I could join the club.

From my perch, I could see everyone. Every arm flailed in an arc, and not always the same one Marla's did -- it could have been an auction with everyone trying to get their bid in. Bea and her husband were practically bouncing in their chairs, to the beat of the music; thank heaven they weren't that heavy. As for my moves, they were pretty much on track. Marla yelled, "Go, Deedie!" between her calls.

I thought back to our first conversation when Marla told me about Zumba. It was only one of a string of careers she's had, she said. She'd always been a musician--- singer, flute, guitar – you name it. But she'd also taught and been a director of plays. Now it was Zumba. Arms up, arms down.

Legs flailing to the left, then out front. Put your chin out, shoulders up, get with it all, it's all so good. Elbows to the sky, elbows down below. Thrust out those arms and throw them up and over. I was panting. And then it was time to wiggle just a little.

Everyone was wiggling a little, just like the Aunt Til had. And laughing. Having fun.

You can get a taste of Zumba at Anne Hathaway's the day after this one by going to https://www.youtube.com/watch?v=Yuop6SQSXfw

Aunt Til's Golden Cheese Puff

(The two secrets to this dish are cheap bread and expensive cheese)

- 8 slices of bread (Wonder bread or some other cheap product)
- ½ pound of good cheddar cheese (Tillamook's sharp is terrific)
- 4 eggs
- 2 cups milk
- 1 t dry mustard
- 1 t Worcestershire
- ¾ t salt (can be omitted or reduced if cheese is good)

Cayenne pepper or hot sauce to taste

1. Grease 9 by 13 dish. Trim crusts from bread, butter with soft butter and cut into fourths.
2. Place a layer of bread in bottom of baking dish buttered side up, leaving space between the small pieces.
3. Add a layer of cheese and then another layer of bread topped with a second layer of cheese.
4. Beat eggs, add milk and seasonings.
5. Pour over bread and cheese.

Refrigerate overnight. Return casserole to room temperature in the a.m. and bake at 325 about an hour.

Plunging Inn...Our Transition

The former horse stalls and pigpens in a century-old bank barn had been transformed into cozy bedrooms, each with its own scent and color palette. We had no idea this is what awaited us at Pretty Gardens Inn. Five miles from anywhere, on an unnumbered country road, the innkeeper who doubled as chief interior designer, met us at the door and breathlessly told how she'd made her B&B dream come true. Her hair curled tight close to her head by a permanent permanent, Mrs. Roeder wore the kind of gingham apron that totally covers up what's underneath, sensible shoes and surprising bright-blue knee socks dotted by Kermit the Frog. "I can show you all the rooms because we don't happen to have any guests right now," she said by way of welcome.

The bubbling cinnamon aromatherapy pot brewed away on the dresser in the first room, dominated by an antique brass bedstead with a cinnamon-hued coverlet. Big red apples accented the dark tan dust ruffle and curtains. The creativity of the color combination stunned my aesthetics.

That earthy aroma and colors provided a startling contrast to the lavender and lace room we visited next. "This one's my favorite," our hostess said as she switched on the purple night lights. "I did it in remembrance of my grandmother," she said, standing solemn as a preacher. A life-size likeness of that rather stern grandmother peered down from the head of the bed. I bet myself her name was Myrtle.

"She looks a little like *my* grandmother," I said. "So pretty." (If my sister had been with us, I couldn't help thinking, she would have nudged me and begun to do some snickering in an effort to get me to do the same.) David nodded his head for some reason.

At the end of the hall came a room with a cabbage-patch doll theme. No scent accompanied it – though I guess it could've been sauerkraut – but dolls, many of which we learned had been handcrafted by Mrs. Roeder herself, inhabited every nook, cranny and surface, everywhere you looked – on the bed, the window seat, the chaise lounge, the dresser, peaking down from the soffit. The story of the soft cotton stuffed Cabbage Patch dolls seeped back into my mind, remembering the year our youngest daughter Sara wanted nothing but one. If you bought one at Toys-"R"-Us, you got the adoption papers along with its given name, all of which were not just unusual, but intentionally tasteless, or so it seemed to me. Farica Scarlett, Cherry Cathyleen, Laraine Cammie, Ariel Leila, Derek Edric, Lucette Jacynth. One was better than another.

"Guests love this room," she said. "We have people who come back to it year after year. And of course since I made each of those kids with my own hands, I also got to name them." As she began introducing each doll by name, I carefully avoided eye contact with David and thanked heaven again my sister wasn't along.

"What do your guests do for entertainment when they visit?" I said right after we'd met Candace Carline (who was wearing a poodle skirt). "Your gardens are quite lovely, but I do wonder what else draws people to your area. Hiking? Antiquing?"

"To tell you the truth, it's Three Mile Island. You know, the nuclear plant that melted down. It's less than a mile away," she started enthusiastically. "You just follow our road right down to the river and you can see it from there. Some days they allow visitors; our guests find it fascinating, especially since the accident. And of course, there are plenty of Amish farms around here. Some of them welcome visitors and even sell quilts and jams and relishes. Have you ever had chow-chow?"

"I have," David said. "My family's Pennsylvania Dutch.

But, Three Mile Island! Not long after the meltdown, David had become Governor Dick Thornburgh's press secretary. The Governor was hailed as a leader who did everything right during the crisis. David was often his spokesman about the experience, forcing him to become something of an expert. Would he want to use that background to entertain guests at this B&B? And what about me? I'd spent years advocating against *all* things nuclear. The very thought of living in the shadow of a large and failed nuclear system, not to mention the specter of radiation sickness, made my stomach go kerplollop.

As we were leaving, Mr. Roeder said, "This B&B takes a lot of upkeep, I'll tell you that. But I bet you're a great handyman, aren't you?" He winked toward David.

David looked up. "Actually, I'm not that good a handyman. In fact, I wouldn't even call myself a handyman. Not at all." Mr. Roeder had no idea, I'm sure, that the message he was getting was for me, and not him.

I decided not to say a word, but Mrs. Roeder filled the gap caused by David's statement by saying, "But I bet you know how to iron, Deedie. If there's anything we do a lot of here besides cooking and fixing, it's ironing."

That damn handyman issue.

Back in the car, we laughed and joked about sending guests to see the melted nuclear reactor and Cabbage Patch dolls. During our drive, David suggested we confine our search to inns located in *destinations*. I couldn't help being astonished at his enthusiasm for a new approach to our next chapter. How could it be that the B&B idea had moved to the front burner so swiftly?

One identifiable trait about the Runkels is they make decisions quickly, sometimes without realizing it. For years, our friends amazed us with their emphasis on discernment and due diligence before making a move; they even had advisors and spreadsheets. We shocked them right back with our alacrity.

"Look how many of our friends came to stay with us in Belize," he said. "We hardly had a week free. . . that's what I mean about how important it is to be a destination."

"Should we think about going back to Belize?" I asked. We'd lived there for almost four years when I was Peace Corps director, and we certainly knew the country well. "Maybe we could find a B&B for sale there."

"No. I don't think we want to be that far away from our kids, do we?" David asked. "But I admit it was great fun having everyone come, making all the arrangements, fixing local food."

I looked over and saw a happier man than I'd seen in a long time. My hand went back to his thigh and patted it.

Even though I would never have a very tight permanent, wear Kermit socks or send people to an irradiated island (from a possibly irradiated site), and I really hated Cabbage Patch dolls, I could definitely imagine myself having the same job as Mrs. Roeder.

The word "job" hung over our heads at that time, a specter of imagined disgrace. We'd both been unemployed before, but never at the same time. Our unemployment status had come about most unexpectedly. Within weeks of each other, both our jobs had come to a screeching halt. David's position, as director of communications for the House of Representatives' Committee on Banking and Finance, had run afoul of Congressional term limits for committee chairs. And my job as executive director of the national organization, Peace Links, ended because its founder decided our method of preventing nuclear war had gone out of style (even though we'd been eminently successful to this very day).

We are not planners, especially not financial planners. We'd always managed to get ourselves pretty good jobs and make pretty good money, but none of it was socked away in a Rainy Day Unemployment Account.

We had no Plan B or back-up professions, e.g. I am not a registered nurse and David is not a lawyer. Our situation was particularly daunting because we knew that being 60 was a big negative. In spite of all our experience and energy, prospective employers saw only dollar signs when they read our resumes. Our earnings history had become a liability rather than an asset, a minus, not a plus -- to our surprise, we'd become expensive commodities over the years, David making over $100K and me not far behind. With our youngest still in college, we simply had to keep on earning money, some-how, some way. We'd never been quite so unhappy. Even though our unem-ployment did not come about because of anything either of us did wrong -- it really *was* circumstances beyond our control -- our joint self-esteem was in the pits. So thunderstruck were we that the sleepless nights and profound ill feelings had begun to seep into our relationship. We weren't being particularly nice to each other. My desk was upstairs and his was downstairs and the twain met mostly by email.

We both went to interviews for possibly perfect jobs. And were called back. But then not called back. Helpful friends invited us to cocktail par-ties so we could network, but we both were so intimidated by our lack of employment status that our tongues tied themselves into square knots. I came down with shingles. David rented a chipper and spent days chop-ping up all of our yard detritus and the neighbors' too. (I don't think they realized it was therapeutic chipping.) For some reason, we didn't have the habit nor the words to talk about our mutual unhappiness; I think we were both afraid that if we talked about it, we'd be even more unhappy. I was considering an act of homicide for the next person who wanted to discuss their experience with one door closing causing another to open. That was bullshit as far as I was concerned.

Ultimately, we decided to join the ranks of Washington consultants, despite the fact that the city has almost more consultants per square inch than springtime cherry blossoms in the Tidal Basin. Silver Communications, Inc. was founded in our dining room over dinner one evening, with the help of a bottle of not-so-good (but affordable) wine. Using our massive rolodexes and our Godson's willingness to fold and lick hundreds of announcement envelopes, we began harvesting. If we were stacking hay bales from our harvest, the animals would barely have survived.

AARP's monthly *Bulletin* signed us on to each write a monthly column about happenings at the state level. The Business and Professional Women's organization and the National Peace Corps Association hired me to work on their publications and meetings. David took on a job as an elementary and high school substitute teacher. We finally had the mortgage covered.

A marketing ploy helped pull us out of our sadness slump and propel us back to what we liked to do and were good at -- hosting dinner parties. Tonight we were having one to "cultivate contacts."

Even though we'd been snarking at each other all day, as we got into the rhythm of our prep work, the tide changed. We started chatting. I heard myself singing, "Oh, What a Beautiful Morning," a traditional pre-party theme song in our house. We admitted to being excited to see how *this* group of friends and acquaintances would get along. We had a reputation as good party hosts and more than a measure of confidence in our abilities in the hospitality arena. Our exhilaration of success in at least *this* realm had us believing in ourselves again, however briefly. Soon we were dancing through our preparations. As I would move toward the oven, David would slide out of the way. He'd head for the 'fridge, and I'd scrunch against the island to let him by. At one pass, he caught my hand and twirled me around in a pirouette. I smiled. We could be in a movie, we looked and felt so good. The kitchen we'd remodeled was full of light and wood. A perfect set.

Minutes before guests were to arrive, David paused to look directly at me for the first time that day. "Would you like a glass of 'cooking wine?'" He smiled, invoking a routine that's gone on between us for years.

"Oh, yes, I'd love some. How great of you to offer."

"Will it be red or white tonight?"

I *never* have anything but white, but the rule is I always have to think of a good reason before I'm granted my wish. "Hmm. I think since we're having fish, I'll have white tonight."

I lifted my glass to my favorite sommelier.

"Listen, honeybun, I'm serious, with a B&B we would be doing what we love to do every day, and earning money for it. Whaddaya think?" The B&B idea was a recurring one. I raised it whenever I found another really unusual salt and pepper set. We would need more than a few if we had a B&B, for heaven's sake.

"I think I hear people at the door right now. And besides, you know I'm not a good enough handyman to be an innkeeper," he said, leaving to welcome our first guests.

I had no idea where his sense that he had to be a good handyman had come from. Was it just the only excuse he could think of? We didn't know any innkeepers, and had never seen a job description for an innkeeper, so I couldn't figure out why he was so concerned about it. In fact, we'd never even been *inside* a B&B before. Our one preparation was my collection of salt and pepper shakers.

Months later, we were halfway home from a family Thanksgiving dinner in Pennsylvania when David pulled a tiny crumpled piece of newspaper out of his pocket.

"I was thinking we ought to at least look at this B&B I saw advertised for sale."

I'd been dozing, partly to stave off the feelings of dread washing over me. Tomorrow would be another day in my home office trying to seem and feel like I was busy at the work of Silver Communications. We had a new contract to promote a movie about the Pope. Neither of us was particularly enthusiastic about it except for the additional income. With the holidays nearly at hand, I couldn't imagine how we were going to afford to send cards, buy gifts, cook the roast beef and all the rest. The Christmas drill at our house is packed with tradition and fun, but what would it be like this year? How would we afford it? Another hundred or so miles and I'd have to face it.

Mr. and Mrs. Roeder had given us a lot to think about. Finally, we had an exhilarating and exciting vision of what we could be and do, though very few hard facts about whether it was even "doable" financially. The goal became to find a location that people wanted to come to, and for reasons David and I could relate to. Several places on the National Historic Register were for sale. One in Boonsboro, Maryland, had been a field hospital during the Battle of Antietam became our first "destination" visit. The capacious dining room looked out on the field where the battle had ended, leaving *23,000* dead.

Trying to turn our attention away from the unfathomable tragedy there, I said to David, "You'd look cute in britches if we had to dress in period costumes."

"You'd be hot in those long skirts, especially if they had hoops," he said.

The next morning, we were lying in bed at the Antietam Inn, feeling dismayed that this place too wasn't our cup of tea. I had admitted the night before that the prospect of talking about the Civil War endlessly would be hard for a girl like me who had worked for peace so long. I didn't go down to breakfast.

From there we were off to the Eastern Shore of Maryland, not far from where we spent our beach vacation every year. But this was a 250-year-old house along a river, down a two-mile driveway. Who would come *here*, we wondered as the wheels of our aging Volvo grated along on the loose gravel?

The owner greeted us in oil-stained overalls, filthy from head to toe. "If you're interested in being innkeepers, I hope you're ready for some hard work," he said. "I've been under the big house all morning doing some repairs to the pumps. Sorry for my appearance. Let's go inside. It's gonna take a while to show you this whole property."

This proved to be our shortest stay, as David spoke first. "We only have about five minutes before we have to leave, but I wonder what you can tell us about the financials of running this operation," he said.

"What you're basically getting here is a lifestyle. Nice house. Country Club dues tax deductible. Meet nice people. Close to the beach, a lot of pumps to repair." he said.

David nudged my elbow back toward the car, and we left with barely a good bye.

Silence reigned for about five minutes as we made our way to the main road. Finally, David said, "Maybe we should consider Ashland. The Oregon Shakespeare Festival is certainly a destination, we both love the theatre, and even better, it's halfway between Lucy in San Francisco and Marsh in Portland. Wouldn't it be great to be that close to them? Let's go online when we get home and see what's for sale there."

"Oregon! You're right, it would be perfect. Remember how much we loved it when we spent the night there last year? It's chock full of B&Bs. Maybe we could get Sara to move there too," I added, thinking how great it would be to have all three of our children on the same coast.

We definitely had loved Ashland. It was the centerpiece of a six-week round-the-country tour we took to reconnoiter with friends and family and our new unemployed status. It reminded us both of our hometowns -- full of eclectic architecture and people, exceptional trees and flowers, all kinds of shops. And oh, the theatre. Two mountain ranges -- the Cascades and Siskiyous -- hovered over the valley where Ashland nestled. A life without the bustle of the beltway and hustle of the Capital city was one we didn't even imagine during the 22 years we lived there, but now, now it seemed like a mecca.

Back in our home offices, each day new items would appear on our respective pro and con lists. Were we really thinking about doing *this*? Did we have the nerve? Friends were skeptical. We'd have to be nice to people *all the time*. It was *really hard* work. It was *business* and neither of us had ever had any experience whatsoever with *business* (until Silver Communications). What about *retirement?* How would we ever afford it? Would there be a Friends' Meeting there? Our Quaker meeting was a big part of our lives. What did you really have to *know* to be an innkeeper besides being nice, cooking breakfast and managing? And surely we could always find a handyman to do projects David couldn't do. I reminded him at dinner one night how good he was at re-wiring lamps and doing chipping, those two things alone proved to me he was handy. More than one friend expressed incredulity that I, who had never eaten an egg in her life, would be destined to fixing one egg dish after another, day after day. And what about the *money?* How much could we get for our house and how much would we have to pay for a B&B? Could we even afford to be thinking about all this?

Fortunately, the Washington area real estate market is almost always "hot." One call to a local realtor reassured us we would walk away from a sale with enough cash to buy an inn.

That night, we called the children and told them this was serious. We really were thinking about picking up stakes and moving across the country.

"Hooray," Marsh and Lucy said in unison.

"It's high time you got out of Washington, both of you," Marsh said. "It's killing you. Besides, if you're out here, we can see you more."

"And eventually we'll get Sara back out here," Lucy said.

The next morning, sitting in my upstairs office, I got mail -- from David. "Have a look at 'The Mousetrap Inn' online. I think it's what we want." I went running down to his office, without even looking it up. We were both finally at the same place at the same time. In our customary way, we were "on it."

I'm not sure why exactly we were both so quick on the trigger, no matter what the issue before us was. Maybe it was David always being on deadline when he was a reporter or me being at the beck and call of various bosses. At any rate, we were seasoned experts at jumping, diving, hopping, bounding, hurtling into action.

The Mousetrap Inn, as pictured online, met our expectations about what an inn owned by the Runkels might look like. From what we saw, there would be no problem making it Runkelesque.

Marshall was willing to drive the five hours down to Ashland from Portland to have a look at the Mousetrap Inn. We found it even more beguiling when our friend Ben speculated that the name had come from the title of the play-within-a-play in *Hamlet*. At the end of the weekend, Marsh filed a five-star report, saying the Inn was just the kind of place where we could thrive.

Walking through the Mousetrap a few days later, I couldn't believe we'd raised a son who would think we'd spend all we had on it. Sponge art appeared everywhere, evidently a decorating theme that inspired the current owner, along with garish polyester quilts and plaid towels. The suspicious little brown spot on the bathroom floor, which David diagnosed as a mouse dropping, was the least of our concerns. We'd come with checkbook prepared to make a down payment and left immediately after breakfast, dismayed and disappointed. Maybe Marsh was just too eager for us to come West.

The realtor drove us to see another inn for sale. All three of us talked nervously the whole way across town, five minutes that seemed more like twenty. The realtor was saying she thought Anne Hathaway's would be more to our liking, especially since we were Easterners. We weren't sure what that meant. David wanted us to know he'd discovered that the reason for the name of the Inn we just left was not Shakespeare but the fact that every mousetrap in the world used to be made across the street from the Inn. I driveled on in the meantime about mouse turds and sponge art.

Anne Hathaway's Cottage, which *was* named after Shakespeare's wife, sat on a rise overlooking East Main Street, half a block from the main drag. A big boxy grey and white house with maroon trim, it looked like a house we could live in (unlike where we'd just come from). A library full of books greeted us, bordered by great tall windows and a window seat right out of my grandmother's dining room. The current owner gave us the business rundown, to which we listened dumbly. The realtor told us we should be as impressed as she was. We were mostly glad there was a business report, but couldn't really relate to its details. The seller and his wife were more than ready to sell, tired of the enterprise after eight years. The realtor said this was a long time for innkeepers to "last."

"What happens to them?" I asked.

"Oh, for some, it just becomes too much of a chore," the realtor said, smiling.

"You'll find out. You'll love it, though," the owner said.

Out of a tiny awkward silence that included shifting of feet and eyes on five people, David blurted, "Let's get on with this sale."

With a plane to catch first thing the next morning, we spent the rest of the day signing an offer, a counter offer and waiting. Our realtor specialized in B&Bs and prattle, so there was no end of talking and we didn't have to do it. We drove around town looking at what had just become our seventh home base. By the end of the day, we'd signed a contract and met with a banker. Three short months stood between that day and our proposed move across the country.

Our friends in Washington and elsewhere on the East Coast couldn't conceal their astonishment when we announced we had done the deed and were actually leaving to do something so "daring." Some outright doubted we would ever make it as "business people," saying we'd probably end up giving away rooms. Others couldn't believe we were taking on a "service" job -- "Do you realize all you're going to be doing is *serving* people?" was a regular refrain – it'll be like being full-time waiters, they said.

Still others expressed outright envy of our getting out of a city that had just survived being a terrorist target barely a year earlier. "No dirty bombs to worry about out that way," David's former boss said.

24

Undeterred, we began sorting through a lifetime of possessions to see which among them would be tucked into a moving truck for the trip cross-country. Our children laid claim to chairs, chests and beds we would no longer need, having purchased an inn full of beds, chests and chairs.

We put our house on the market one day and it sold the next. We were set.

For our Christmas card that year, I called upon Shakespeare to explain our determination to go into "service," as some referred to our new career. Since our guests are drawn to Ashland by the Bard, what did *he* have to say about service? Plugging in the words "Shakespeare's servants," this is what I came up with:

A servant appears in every play in the canon, perhaps as living proof that unconditional love is ever-present, lest we forget that.

A *re*-creation story was the theme of our Christmas story in 2001. We were re-creating ourselves, and how perfect to undertake it in the 38th year of our marriage as two people committed to *unconditional love.* Not a bad life choice, we figured. More than that, it helped in the recovery of our self-worth that had been so undermined by unemployment, or under-employment. With some help from a therapist, I'd begun to understand how important being appreciated by others was to both of us -- we weren't particularly good at generating that kind of appreciation for ourselves. If we did it right as innkeepers, we'd be showered in kudos everyday. And we'd have *jobs.* And we'd be our own bosses. We rode the crest of newfound purpose, fueled by the prospect of this massive change we'd wrought. The exhilaration of it kept us awake some nights, totally consumed with the extrication process.

The last twisting and descending the final mountain before Ashland fell on July 3rd. We were determined not to miss Ashland's iconic Fourth of July parade. Our cross-country trip had been punctuated by quick visits as we went Westward. David's Mom in Western Pennsylvania, old friends in Madison, a motel night or two. We wasted little time. Everything that didn't fit in the moving van filled our new green Passat station wagon to the brim. Poor Hattie, our chocolate lab, had to squeeze her ample body into a third of the back seat.

The panorama splayed out before us could not have been more divine – mountains covered with evergreens, canyons of rock and once-molten lava, distant peaks and buttes rising and rolling over it all. Overwhelmed by the fact that this landscape was becoming my new backyard, I took off my seat belt and poked my head out the open sunroof. A whoop of celebration came from my deepest recesses. How could we be so lucky? "Yahoo, here we are, here we are!" I called at the top of my lungs. Hattie sat up, wagging her tail (as best she could in cramped space) and wondering what had come over her mother. David joined in, waving out the sunroof to all those trees. He patted my bottom and I wiggled it for all that flora and fauna to see.

Crossing the threshold of 586 East Main Street the evening before it was to become ours, we held hands and kissed. Here we were, finally. We'd already been thoroughly delighted with the Fourth of July parade, cheering on the sidelines then following the human drift to Lithia Park for an old-fashioned carnival. We happened to fall in right behind Jesus Christ carrying a very large cross and some very small twirlers from the Y. We needed none of the constantly-proffered encouragement from our realtor -- we were sold as townspeople and soon we'd be businesspeople. I looked around warily, hoping not to see some massive flaw we'd missed in our exuberance months earlier. In one of the B&B books I'd skimmed in the bookstore, I'd read about new owners finding a drooping ceiling in a room they'd forgotten to look in.

"Might you be interested in a scone lesson tomorrow morning?" the soon-to-be-former owner asked. "I remember you saying you've never made them."

"Sure," I said. "What time?"

"6:45 sharp," he said curtly.

As we left, we looked back at this big old house about to be ours that had been built as a Boarding House and was on the Historic Register. "We have jobs. We're innkeepers," I said.

"Beginning for you at 6:45 tomorrow morning," David said, grabbing my hand.

Less than 24 hours later, we were at the bank signing the final papers. Between signatures the about-to-be former owner imparted last-minute counsel on how to do business. "You've got to get the guest's money up front, or you'll get stiffed. Teatime? Put out a few cookies. At breakfast, don't serve any meat. No one likes it anymore and besides, it's expensive." He seemed more than a little concerned about our business acumen. *Had he talked to our friends?* "And never pay more than minimum wage if you want to keep your bottom line healthy." Anne Hathaway's was going to be rather different under the Runkels, I wanted to say but didn't.

"Is there enough food in the kitchen for tomorrow's breakfast?" I asked. It suddenly occurred to me we'd need food. Why hadn't we thought of that?

"You'll have to check. That's something you want to keep a close eye on -- eggs and milk and that sort of thing. I know they're oranges, flour and sugar. But welcome to innkeeping, folks!" he said. He smiled a smile I considered vicious, but I think that judgment came from my fragile state.

When we welcomed new guests that afternoon at 3:00, they instantly wanted to know what had happened to the former owner.

"He sold the inn to us," we said confidently. "Today. Just this morning." Zeroing in on one of them, I asked the question that would become our gold standard: "And what do you do when you're not coming to Ashland?"

"I'm a lawyer in Dallas," he said. Then turning to my co-owner, "So, Dave, you must be a pretty good handyman."

Drat! Don't start about the handyman, please.... I looked over at David, his special jovial smile spread across his face. "You'd be amazed at all I can do," he said confidently. I looked over and smiled back.

It didn't take long for David to have a chance to show his skills.

The following morning would be our very first B&B breakfast, which included the elements that would become our daily formula – scones, fruit, meat and main course. As we sat in the kitchen planning, I looked around for the cookbooks we'd brought. "Didn't you put them in one of the boxes in the car?" I asked.

"I thought you had," David said.

"Oh good lord," I said. "Let me look in this envelope. He said they'd left their recipes for us." I feverishly sorted through little scraps of paper with nearly-unreadable scribbles on them. "Aha!"

David was squeezing oranges when I returned and showed the recipe for German Apple Pancake to him.

"Let's call it "Will's Favorite Pancake." Doesn't that sound more authentic from Anne Hathaway's kitchen?" he suggested.

The guests loved it, especially its name. And they also loved the bacon. Having ignored the former owner's counsel, we weren't totally surprised there wasn't a single piece left on the huge platter we served. We knew bacon was irresistible.

Cooking and serving breakfast for twelve was a lot more challenging than a dinner party, we discovered that morning. Arriving in the kitchen before seven, I had my first scone lesson while David worked on the fruit course, coffee and orange juice. Once my scone lesson was over, David began assembling the main course while I set the table. *Why weren't there enough napkins to match this tablecloth? Why didn't they have more tablecloths?* Practically before we knew it, the clock hit nine. With help from Cicily, a young staff member, we began putting out the fruit plates, filling coffee mugs, pouring juice. By the time we finished doing that, it was time to begin putting the main course plates together. I'd collected nasturtiums from the garden to put on each one and showed Cicily how I wanted it done. Oh my heavens, they were already done eating! Time to clear the table. I told Cicily she'd won the chance to begin loading the dishwasher while I went out to talk to guests, or what we've come to call, "chat 'em up."

Walking into the living room, I beheld David and the Texas lawyer in an unlikely standoff. Each had a hand on a toilet plunger suspended between them, the same thing you do with a bat when you're deciding who bats first. "Here's the plunger you asked for," David was saying, as he gently pushed the plunger toward our guest.

"Well, yes, we *do* need a plunger in our bathroom," said the lawyer, "But the way I figure, it may be my poop, but it's your toilet." And he pushed the plunger back at David.

"I guess you're right, there," David said, accepting the plunger.

Apparently we'd just had our first introduction to one of what would be countless "The Guest is Always Right" situations.

That evening we collapsed on an air mattress in the apartment we'd rented a few blocks from the inn. Our situation was just short of camping, since the moving truck with our bed and furniture (and the cook books) hadn't arrived yet. Our long-term plan was to move into the back suite at the inn, but for the rest of the summer it had been reserved for guests. David reached over to touch my hand and asked if I'd like a glass of cooking wine.

"I thought you'd never ask," I said.

"Red or white?"

"I'm too tired for red. Let's have white tonight."

He returned from the kitchen with two jelly jars of my favorite Sauvignon Blanc. I took a sniff, then lifted my glass to him. "We've done it. Here's to my favorite plunger!"

Will's Favorite Apple Pancake

(Better if batter is made the night before)

- 4 eggs
- 1 cup milk
- 2 T melted butter
- 1 t vanilla

- ½ cup flour
- 1 T sugar
- ½ t baking powder
- ¼ t nutmeg
- pinch salt

1. Whip eggs and add milk, butter and vanilla. Mix dry ingredients together and slowly whisk into the wet mixture. Refrigerate overnight.

2. In the morning, preheat oven to 425. On stovetop melt half stick of butter in a cast iron skillet, brush up sides of pan, leave on low heat or turn off.

3. Mix together half to two/thirds cup of sugar (according to how sweet you like it), half teaspoon of cinnamon, and a quarter teaspoon of nutmeg. Core, peel and slice in thin pieces of two small apples (We love to do this with peaches and pears also).

4. Turn on heat and sprinkle half the sugar mixture into buttered skillet. Arrange the apple slices and sprinkle the rest of the sugar on top. Cook several minutes until mixture bubbles. Turn off the heat and gently pour the batter over the apples.

5. Transfer the pan to the oven and bake for 15 minutes on the bottom or middle rack at 425, then 5 or so minutes at 375.

Cut into wedges and serve hot.

Blue Sapphire Scones

"**N**ever touch the dough."

I felt like I was back in Mr. Smith's Chemistry lab, scene of my very first C in high school. My mentor, about to be the former owner, might as well have been the Sergeant of a battalion of rookie innkeepers doing basic training for all of his authority. My intimidation level was so high I couldn't make the Cuisinart close properly.

"We're known for our scones, and we've worked hard to perfect this recipe, so I strongly recommend you stick by it," he said intently, scooping out the pastry flour. Holding the Pyrex measuring cup up to eye level, he looked at me through the glass. *Was he making sure I was paying attention?*

There's something about this teaching method that completely disempowers me. Even though I wanted to be a champion scone maker, this guy seemed intent on making it so intimidating that I was sure to screw up. His encouraging words hit my ears and bounced into the patronizing bin. Here he was, nice enough to be training me, but the more he talked, the less trained I felt.

"We order the pastry flour from the Co-op in 25-pound bags. It takes about a week after you order to arrive, so running out is something you don't want to do," he said. "Don't wait until the last minute. Also, notice that the bag has an orange stripe on it so you don't confuse it with regular flour." Fear and awe were taking over any sense of confidence I might have

31

brought with me that day. *How did he know I always pushed deadlines? And whatever was the difference between pastry and regular flour, anyway. Who cared, besides him?* This job seemed like it was mostly common sense, but he was making it sound *hard, if not impossible.* My ability to feel instantly insecure proved to be a particular liability this morning.

"You've got to keep in mind that you're working in a commercial kitchen now and can't risk doing *anything* that might jeopardize your guests' health. Germs are everywhere, *everywhere*! No matter how thoroughly you wash your hands, you know they have microbes on them that could have the whole house vomiting in no time."

He emptied the flour into the big bowl of the Cuisinart and took up the white plastic spatula from its precise position next to the medium stainless knife. I was busy thinking about guests with projectile vomiting as I watched him begin scraping the scone mixture off the side of the bowl. His lecture continued. "Just think how often nurses, doctors, dentists take off their gloves and put on new ones – that tells you something, doesn't it?" He held my gaze for a moment. I was beginning to feel as sick as those guests of mine were surely going to be. *Should I get gloves like the ones I had to use when I volunteered at the soup kitchen or surgical ones?*

"Hm-hm," I nodded, wondering why I hadn't thought of that myself. My hair was as white as his so I certainly had lived long enough to know such things. But he had a degree in chemistry from Cornell. What would an English major from Penn State know? *Somehow my Ivy League-State University inferiority complex had managed to discover me in Anne Hathaway's 100 year-old kitchen.*

Once the dough had coalesced, my teacher deftly turned it out onto the cutting board and shaped it into a log, patting one end and then the other, with the spatula, of course. I couldn't help thinking how ridiculously labor-intensive this process seemed when all you really needed to do was get your hands, germ-laden as they may be, around that dough. After cutting the log into quarters, he separated out one portion.

"Okay, I know you can do this part," he said. I stepped up, still feeling like a not-very-smart school girl, certain he'd just read my mind, full as it was with unsanitary, possibly poisonous thoughts.

"Pat this into a circle, or a wheel. Maybe four and a half inches, maybe four and three quarters in diameter." *Did I need a tape measure? Would I use my hands for this step?* He handed me the spatula.

I took it and began patting and patting. I knew if I could get my hands on that dough, it would do just exactly what it should. But then the guests would be dead.

"A left-hander, eh? You people have a hard time in the kitchen, I've heard." *What are you talking about?* "Give it a little more oomph, Deedie. Go ahead," he said. *I could feel perspiration developing and it wasn't from exercise. I was beginning to feel a little harassed around the edges.*

My laborious spatula patting complete, he said, "Now cut that into quarters and lift them -- gently, now -- on to this cookie sheet," he said. "The oven's ready – and by the way, don't ever try to put them in if it hasn't reached 450 or they'll be hard as rocks."

"Oh sure," I said. "Preheating. I know about *that*. I'm just worried it's taking me too long."

"Time is definitely a concern, but if you put more muscle into your spatula, it'll go much faster." *Maybe I needed to lift more weights.*

As he prepared the jam pots to serve with the scones, he went on. "We run a pretty tight ship here. We've learned it's essential to keep things on time. *On time.* The guests expect it." This last dictum sounded like a giant challenge to me. *We hadn't signed the papers yet. Maybe we should rethink this whole notion. But what would we tell the kids? Our friends? What would we tell ourselves, for Heaven's sake?*

My professor of scones disappeared into the dining room with "our" scones. I was happy to be by myself for a moment. He'd brought a sheaf of *Instructional Memos*, as he called them, and I was eager to read them.

"She made them all by herself." From the kitchen, I could hear him talking to the guests. He'd delivered the lightly browned scones with just a few minutes to go before eight o'clock.

"But they taste and look just like *yours*," one of the guests said.

"I was just her supervisor," he said. *Why did he lie like that?* "Rest assured, she did the job, cut those scones in perfect triangles, and I think she's launched as a successful innkeeper. What do you think? Good enough to eat, aren't they?"

Why couldn't he have been that nice to me?

"Absolutely," I heard one man with a Southern drawl say. "I'm not even that much of a scone man myself, but I'm ready for a second. When are you going to introduce us to our new innkeeper?"

"Deedie, come on out here and meet your guests," he called.

I'd been in the kitchen reviewing the extensive notes left for us by *Mrs. Naval Officer*. How to fold a towel correctly: Smooth it out and put your arm flat on the towel so no crows' feet develop at the fold. Be sure your hands are perfectly clean. *Is this for real? Is she serious? Who would notice? And I thought crow's feet were the emerging wrinkles at the corner of my eyes.* How to polish the silver. *I've been doing that since I was six.* How to fold a pillowcase and a sheet. Again, the fear of crow's feet. *Why would anyone take the time to write such things down?* On some level, I knew I should feel exceptionally lucky to have their help – but was this really what innkeeping was all about? It's true, we hadn't done much preparing for our new career earlier. We'd skimmed a book or two on the subject and found them boring. We'd done some online research for maybe about ten minutes. And even talked to probably half a dozen innkeepers, most of them so eager to sell their place to us and get out of the business that they made it all seem dreamy. A friend had given us a whole set of *Fawlty Towers*, a British comedy about a B&B. Nowhere was precision towel folding mentioned.

"You're a good scone maker, Deedie, I can tell," one of the guests (an old regular, I'd been briefed) said graciously when I appeared.

"Oh you won't know if I've mastered them until tomorrow morning when my coach isn't around," I smiled a wan smile -- a smile that was not altogether genuine. In fact, it was full of fear that this time tomorrow, they'd all be coming down with paramecium fever, or something like that. *I couldn't help thinking my mentor was going home to tell his wife I was a dismal failure.*

As it turned out, the next morning's guests were treated to scones that turned into stone minutes after leaving the oven, which had been perfectly pre-heated, per directions. That night, debriefing with David, I was close to tears.

"When I cleared the table today, there were SIX left of the dozen I put out. That's proof right there that I'm a failure in the scone department. Did you know that the former owner was a chemistry major at Cornell? He talked about the *chemistry* of cooking all morning. And you know chemistry is not one of my strong suits. And when he wasn't talking about chemistry, he sounded like he was an agent from the Centers for Disease Control giving a course on "How to Avoid Killing Your Guests.""

Putting his big hands on my shoulders, David said, "Maybe you just made too many. I think we should both try not to worry – it will only keep us from succeeding." I kept my face buried in his chest until the tears let up a little. Would tomorrow be easier? I couldn't muster the confidence necessary to believe it.

A couple of days later I was working in the office at the rear of the house at our new full-time occupation when someone appeared at the door. I looked up to see a tall, thin man in a dark blue Greek sailor's cap. Dark curls ran around its edge like sewn-on trim.

"Oh. Are you checking in?" I asked, getting up to shake hands. *Had I forgotten someone was scheduled to arrive today?*

"Well, I don't have a reservation, but I wonder if you have a room available," he said, revealing an accent from somewhere Down Under. "With a name like Anne Hathaway's, I figured you had to be a decent enough place."

"We like to think we're a *very* decent place," I said, laughing a nervous laugh, "and as it happens, we do have space." I decided it was best not to mention that we specialized in scones, given the current stone situation, especially not to someone from the British Empire. "How long were you hoping to stay?"

"Oh, perhaps a week. My name's Nigel McLaren. I'm on an extended tour of the U.S., and I've heard quite a bit about the Shakespeare theatre here. Thought I'd catch some plays and get to know your town. How much do you suppose it would come to for a week?"

A week! Most of our bookings were for only two or three days, and a week during the season's slow time was a veritable windfall. New as I was to the business, I was certain a week was something to treasure, for sure. And, I quickly thought, a week's reservation would be worth giving him a break. But David and I hadn't discussed discounts. I tried to do some calculating on my mind's abacus, to no avail. *Oh well, go with your instinct.*

"We'd be happy to give you a 20 per cent discount on what would be over $1,000 dollars, plus tax," I suggested hopefully.

"Oh my heaven," he said.

I couldn't decide if his response was awe at the size of the bill or delight at the discount or what. I was so worried that he wasn't going to book that I almost instantly shot back with, "Well then, how would 25 be?"

"Oh, that's much better than I could *ever* have imagined," Nigel said, putting his hand out to shake on the deal. Our first discount had turned out to be exactly what our DC friends had worried about -- we wouldn't charge enough. With their voices of warning ringing in my mind, I invited Nigel to follow me so I could show him his room.

As we passed through the kitchen, we came upon the six staff members we'd inherited making themselves smoothies with the leftover break-fast fruit. *Was this typical behavior? I'd been raised to always be busy, or at least look busy when the boss came around. They were just feeding them-selves. Maybe that fruit could have been chunked and put out at teatime. I* introduced Nigel and informed them he was a "walk-in" guest who would be staying for a week in the room we now called Hamnet, after one of Shakespeare's children.

The day we became owners of the inn, our first official act was to change the names of the rooms. An inn named for Shakespeare's wife should have rooms named for the people who actually lived with Anne and Will, not boring old Sunflower or Front room or Family Suite. A little bit of research turned up what we needed. The upstairs rooms would bear the names of their children, Hamnet's twin Judith and their older sister Susanna.

"It's a good thing you put him in Hamnet," Colleen said, "because it's the only room ready. Today was such a huge check-out, we still have all the other rooms to clean. It might be a little dusty, though – no one's been in there all week. 'Just thought I'd warn you." *Oh, good Lord. You're not only not working, you're telling the guest his room is dirty!*

"Thanks, Colleen," I offered, glancing at Nigel to gauge his reaction. He nodded at me, and I thought he smiled a little.

As I guided Nigel through the house and up the stairs to his possibly dusty room, I pointed out Mother Mary's room, named for Shakespeare's mother who lived with the family. And Will's Study, a small room I liked to imagine might have resembled the kind of space where all the plays would have been written. Climbing the stairs, I told Nigel the inn's schedule – scones and coffee out at eight, breakfast at nine, tea at four, and late-night after-theatre snacks with port and sherry.

"Do you have any food allergies or restrictions?" I asked.

"No, I don't. My only vice at all is getting up very early in the morning and having a slice of fresh ginger in a cup of very hot water. I brought my own ginger with me from my last stop. All I need is a very sharp knife, which I'm sure you have."

I nodded with confidence. Our knives at home had always been dull. Sensing this about us, the Naval officer had been quick to tell me how important it was to keep our knives sharpened as he introduced me to all of them lined up in rank order on the magnet on the wall, sharp enough to cut nearly everything. My little finger was a test case the first day, leading to a band-aide bundle around my knuckle to keep my blood from giving the guests an acute case of something.

"I'll be in the kitchen quite early making scones," I said. "So just come and find me and I'll set you up. *Scones! Something occurred to me.* "You must be used to scones where you come from?" I said, suddenly feeling nervous. Nigel nodded enthusiastically.

"Here's your room," I said, opening the door of Hamnet and taking a quick look around for signs of dust bunnies. Smoothing the bedspread, I found myself confessing that we were brand new at innkeeping.

"And scones weren't really in my repertoire. But since they're sort of the Anne Hathaway signature offering, I really need to get proficient at it. So far they've seemed more like stones." I had begun to fidget, and as I sometimes do when nervous, reveal more than I should. I ran my fingers through my hair as I felt my body shift into Panic Gear. "People are nice enough to eat some of them, but I'm sure it's because they're hungry and polite. I tell you, once they cool off, we could use them as retaining walls in the garden." *Deedie, shut yourself up!*

"I'm no expert myself," Nigel said. "But I do remember how Gran would pound down that dough as if she was beating a rug. She pounded with one palm and then the other and shaped and then pounded some more and shaped it all into a nice circle she cut in quarters. Does that sound famil-iar?" he said.

"Hmmm, let's talk more about that tomorrow." *Did Nigel's Granny actually use her hands?* "Let me know if you need anything," I said, backing out of the room as politely as I could feeling a surge of confidence and lib-eration scurry through my frontal lobe. If Granny could pound them and Nigel was still alive as proof it wasn't life-threatening, then I could pound away myself.

I hurried downstairs, eager to tell David about our unexpected arrival and possible coaching in the scone department. *Free coaching would make the discount worthwhile, I calculated.* I'd also have to figure out a diplomatic way to tell Colleen that while I very much appreciated her candor, dust just wasn't a subject we discussed in front of guests, particularly when it had to do with a room a guest was about to pay a lot of money for, discount or no discount.

In the kitchen the next morning, I assembled the requisite baking tools and got out Nigel's sharp knife for him. Then I went to the sink to give my hands a scrubbing worthy of the commercial kitchen in which I now worked. As I dried them and headed back to my dreaded task, I glanced down again at my sparkling blue sapphire engagement ring. Nearly 40 years ago, David had presented me with this treasure. At least I had his love and appreciation to support me as I tried my hand – or rather, spatula – once again at scone-making. *Would I have the nerve to do it like Nigel's Granny did? I didn't know for sure.* I applied a new layer or two of band-aides to my finger, worried that Nigel would be shocked to see my ugly little wound uncovered in the kitchen. Who knew, maybe he was an under-cover health inspector.

The tea kettle had just begun to whistle when Nigel came around the corner from the living room. He prepared his morning brew as if he were already quite used to working in a kitchen. "All right if I perch on this lovely stool?" he said.

"Most certainly. But here's the deal -- I want you to help me make scones as good as your Granny's." I explained that I wasn't really convinced the sterile process dictated by the former owner was the key to success and had been quite relieved to hear about his Granny's pounding method.

As Nigel sipped his ginger tea, I cut the cream and egg into the buttered flour and asked him questions about Brisbane, his home city. Wielding my spatula, I cut and folded over and over. A daily swimmer with good biceps for someone my age, I felt my arm wearing out.

"Is this the way you remember your Granny doing it?" I asked my coach.

Nigel looked into the big stainless steel bowl. "If I were you," he said, "at this point I'd get my hands in there. Otherwise, it's going to take you forever."

Hooray! I immediately dropped the spatula, plunged both hands into the dough. That dough must have been happy to be combined by hand because it came together swiftly, almost magically.

"That's exactly what I remember," Nigel said approvingly, nodding his head so vigorously his curly hair bounced. "Doesn't that *feel* right?"

"It sure makes it easier." I lifted the big ball out of the bowl and deposited it on the floured board. *Surely this little contact wouldn't nauseate the guests.* I cut the ball into fourths.

"Now here's where you begin to pound," Nigel said, slapping his hand flat down on the counter three times. "Pound, pound, pound."

David looked over from his orange-squeezing post. "Look, David. I'm making scones just like Nigel's grandmother." Pound! I slapped the dough once, then again.

"I knew you'd figure it out," he called, exercising his own biceps with another pull on the handle of the manual squeezer.

A mere twelve minutes after putting them in the oven, I removed the scones. They looked nothing like the ones I'd made the day before. They'd risen nicely and felt very light as I happily, victoriously lifted each one into a napkin-lined basket.

"Thank you so much, Nigel," I said as I carried them outside to the patio where the guests were waiting for breakfast. I felt like giving him a hug.

"You can thank Granny," he winked.

Breakfast was over practically as quickly as it began -- seconds of the spinach quiche had been offered, along with endless refills of coffee. When David and I stepped out into the garden to join the guests, everyone suddenly stopped talking.

"Here she is! Mrs. Scone," one of the guests announced in a voice worthy of the stage. Everyone started clapping. I could feel myself blushing, suddenly unsure of what to say. Nigel saved the moment by saying, "Today there's a little bit of Australia, and my Granny in the scones."

"What magic did you do today?" Patty said. "These scones just melted in my mouth."

I didn't want to give away the secret in case these folks wouldn't approve of my hands-on, intimate contact with their dough. Before I could construct an answer, she said, "And I wanted to mention something I noticed yesterday. You and I have exactly the same engagement rings. I told my husband last night they must have come from the same jeweler."

She placed her hand on the table to show off her ring – a blue sapphire with a diamond on either side. I placed my considerably older and less tanned hand next to hers. Two tiny diamonds on either side of . . . an empty setting. No sapphire! No sapphire! *It was like an alarm had gone off in my head.*

"Oh my," I gasped, looking up at our guests. I could only imagine where that sapphire was at that very moment. That engagement sapphire was now sailing through the colon of one of these guests, I surmised. I looked over at David, who was shaking his head, a little quizzically. Nigel caught my eye. I shook my head slightly to ward off any speculation in front of the guests about his Granny's scone-making method. He smiled. I smiled back. *Oh my God, not only was I risking contamination of the scones that would sicken the guests, but now they were going to get a bad case of diverticulosis, or whatever it is you get when you eat sapphires. Thank God no one's crown had been cracked, or at least not yet reported as it sashayed through their mouths.*

Patty put her hand on mine and said, "What you need to do is go straight to your jeweler. He'll be able to find you a beautiful substitute. Don't worry. I'm always in and out of my jeweler getting the setting tightened. How often do, er, did – you get yours done?"

Patty was tall and tan and very slim, the very type of woman I'd always wanted to be and never was – I didn't want to reveal that being "in and out" of "my jeweler's" had *never* been on my personal itinerary or routine errands.

I glanced around again at all the concerned faces at the table. "It is a shock, I have to say," I said. "I do remember seeing it when I brushed my teeth this morning." Then, suddenly, not wanting to further trace my steps over the past hour nor the travels of the sapphire, I stopped. "What a great idea, Patty. We'll go right down to the jeweler this afternoon. Thanks. Of course that's what we should do."

Later that day, David and I did walk downtown to drop the ring off at the jeweler. *I was consumed with guilt. Not only was I struggling to make a good scone, I couldn't even keep track of my engagement sapphire. I didn't deserve to have such nice things like a B&B and a sapphire.* The estimate for the new sapphire totaled significantly more than Nigel's tab, which in my twisted way I'd imagined might cancel each other out -- surprise income vs. surprise calamity. *Now we had a jeweler whose first name we knew.* I quickly said, "Rick, there's no rush to get this done. Take as long as you like re-making it." *It would be a long while before we had that kind of money to throw around on new sapphire rings. After all, we needed new towels for the inn, among many other things.*

By the end of our first season, Anne Hathaway's scones had become something to write home about, worth their headline status on our new website. Our Christmas letter recounted that I'd made 1,528 in my first season.

On our first day off after closing the Inn for the winter break, I lay in bed listening to NPR. What a luxury – no need to bound out at 6 a.m. to get breakfast underway.

David arrived with coffee and *The New York Times*, the ultimate morning treat. I turned to my favorite section while David fumbled around in the top drawer of his dresser. Coming over to the bed with a smile on his face, he handed me a small box.

"This is for our 39th anniversary *and* for a world-class scone maker," he said, leaning down to give me a kiss.

The box contained an entirely new engagement ring. A large blue sapphire with a small diamond on either side safely *embedded* in white gold. No need for regular tightening.

"I guess we'll have to take blue sapphire scones off our menu," he said.

Ginger Scones

This recipe has been honed over 15 years and literally thousands of scones. Using one's hands for the shaping step is essential.

Preheat to 450.   Yield: 4 good-size scones

- 1 cup pastry flour
- 1 T+ sugar
- 1 heaping tsp. baking powder
- Pinch of salt
- 1/3 stick *frozen* butter cut up into small cubes
- 1 egg broken into measuring cup.
- Enough heavy cream to make 1/3 C. *total* liquid.

1. Combine dry ingredients in Cuisinart.
2. Dice a very thin slice of a Granny Smith apple and add.
3. Add butter and combine until flour and butter are thoroughly combined, causing well in middle of Cuisinart.
4. Pour dry ingredients into bowl and blend in ginger about ¼ C. of chopped crystallized ginger. If you're making more scones, increase.
5. Beat 1 egg into cream.
6. Create well in dry mix, add all but a smidgeon of liquid mixture.
7. Cut cream into dry mix, moving in a circle, turning bowl until it coalesces. If your arm gets sore, take a break.
8. Shape the dough into a ball using your hands, smoothing the dough.
9. Divide dough in two halves for small scones, keep as one ball for larger ones.
10. Pat into circle(s) about 4" or so in diameter, about ¼" thick.
11. Cut into 4 scones each and place on ungreased cookie sheet.
12. Brush tops with reserved liquid.

Bake 5-6 minutes, then rotate and bake an additional 5-6 minutes

Who Knew?

Our whole entire complete family gathered around the dining room table covered in hibiscus-laden oilcloth at our rented house on Kauai. Sunshine dappled the aqua Pacific a half block away, a neighborly breeze threw the yellow gingham curtains our way. Amidst this postcard serenity, an un-characteristic solemnity hung over the first official meeting of Anne Hathaway's Board of Directors. Our son Marshall, his wife Melissa, our daughter Lucy and her husband Art and our daughter Sara. Ramona, nine months, was napping in the child's room.

That first meeting of our Board occurred on the third day after we all arrived. Intent on making the occasion seem official and business-like, we'd spent the week before we left Oregon preparing. Profit and Loss Statement. Occupancy levels. Marketing budget. Project list. On the plane, we brainstormed an agenda.

The time was set for 2 p.m. We figured lunch would be over and it would make a good pause in the day -- from the sun, shave ice and snorkeling. David and I passed out the P&L statements. We passed out our occupancy levels and projections for the next year. To everyone's surprise, paper shuffling had entered the lexicon of Runkel family lore, replacing the normal boisterous chatting usually present at family gatherings.

I brought the meeting to order without a gavel.

"Do we have an agenda?" Marshall asked. He's a politician.

"Of course we do," I said. "It's just not printed. But you have all those other papers and Dad and I are going to go over them with you right now. Okay?"

"Get on with it, Mom. This is Hawaii," Lucy said.

I looked over at David, who was shaking his head. We had gone over who would cover which items on our hand-printed agenda, but neither of us was feeling particularly confident. I was in our room madly going over the agenda to be certain we'd put a small "d" for me and a large "D" for David under the appropriate topic.

"I'm just going over our assignments," I said.

"Well don't start changing them now," he said. "I've got mine down pat."

"Good for you," I said. Or may have snarled.

Normally good public speakers, on this day, nervousness reigned. My voice shook a little, David stuttered some.

Openly sharing with our closest family the challenges we were facing (which in the deep of night included *failure*) was nearly more daunting than figuring out how we would pay for a new stove, in fact a whole new kitchen? Did we really need new mattresses in every room? Should we advertise? Did we need a new reservation system? How could we develop more business in the winter so we wouldn't have to worry too much, or keep borrowing more money? Nevertheless, we launched into our plans for new construction and other projects; capital improvements, deferred maintenance, possible rate increases and marketing.

Business and financial issues large and small flew at us like a swarm of no-seeums.

As enthusiastic as they'd been about coming to Hawaii, these kids of ours were less than happy about missing time in the sun and did nothing to hide their impatience. Clad in their bathing suits, they didn't look very Board-ly. I'd planned an official Board of Directors meeting photo in case the IRS needed proof of its existence, but alas, hadn't announced a dress code. The co-CEOs were dressed as professionally as possible, wearing shoes, even.

"Why can't we do this later?" Marshall asked.

"Because this is serious -- this is our business. And if you're going to be on the Board, this is information you need. And no beer drinking during the meeting, please," I said.

Five more bored faces have never stared back harder as we worked through the unprinted agenda. Lucy caught my eye at one point and rolled her hands as if she were a basketball referee calling someone for a moving foul. I chomped my jaws together and glared back at her.

"So, we want to hear from you. Any thoughts, feedback, observations? We're serious about wanting to involve you guys in the business, as much as possible, anyway," David said.

I looked around the table. The afternoon rain had started, so maybe they would be more attentive now that they weren't missing the sun. Marshall appeared to be studying the P&L statement, but one couldn't be sure. Lucy was leafing through all the hand-outs. I'd hoped she might be helpful on the staffing table, since workforce development is her field. She might as well have been dealing the cards for gin rummy or answering emails (though I'd outlawed computers and iPhones). Sara stared out the window. Art (the geek in the group) had slyly gotten his iPhone out and was doing calculations, the only one among them who seemed at least a little engaged.

But all was quiet. David looked over at me; I was sure he was thinking *"This wasn't a good idea after all."*

Suddenly awash in doubt, I wondered if we'd been thorough enough. Did they not notice that we'd increased the occupancy by 15% over three years? That we'd ended the year with more money in the bank than we'd *ever* had? And even though we were going to have a hard time getting through the winter with no guests, having a bank balance would look good to lenders when we went out to borrow again. That in no short order, we'd changed Anne Hathaway's *brand* to something that was attracting more advance reservations than there had been in the past? (Though this last was just a hunch because of the lack of records.)

I looked at David again and he did the little grimacing headshake he does when he feels like there's nothing we can do. *It felt like at least a half hour of silence had passed. The rain had stopped.*

Suddenly, the silence was broken.

"Who knewwwwwww?" Lucy exclaimed loudly, finally. "Mom, Dad, how did you do this? You're not business people…at least you *weren't*, but it sure looks like you are now!" She was beaming, her pink cheeks pinker than ever.

"You two definitely deserve a toast," Marshall said. "Look at this. You've taken that old sow's ear of an inn and made it into a successful business, that's for sure. Here, here!"

All of a sudden, they were all on their feet, clapping.

My eyes filled with tears at these totally unexpected votes of confidence. I went over and hugged David and before I was done, we were all hugging each other.

"*Now* you can have some beer," I said. "I'm going to have a vodka and tonic myself."

Reasons some might adjudge facile, if not fickle, underpinned our decision to create a Board of Directors comprised only of our three children and spouses in or close to their forties three years after we started our career as innkeepers: 1. We'd read in a small business handbook we perused at the book store one night on our way home from having drinks downtown that having a group of people function as a sounding board was a worthwhile thing, particularly for rookie business owners. Since we'd both had some experience with Boards of Directors (albeit not commercial ones) we remembered and relished the notion of having access to a group that could advise us and point us in the right direction when we needed help. Despite having a network of other innkeepers with whom we had made friends, we had discovered business operations were at the bottom of the list of things ever discussed when we gathered. Bedspreads and bedbugs (I'm not kidding about this) were far more popular topics. So I guess at the end of the day we were looking for some support from able-bodied people we knew and could trust; 2. Why have our kids? It goes without saying that they're all very smart and would say "yes" if we asked and probably, maybe, we hoped, end up being assets. But the other piece of key information was another fact we'd divined from reading an IRS small business tax information flier entitled "What's Tax Deductible?" *Board of Directors' meeting expenses.* Did this mean that if we appointed the kids to the Board, we could hold the meeting anywhere and charge it off, making it affordable? Hmm, we thought. That might make Christmas presents easy. Hence, stockings that hung with care at the top of Anne Hathaway's stairs that year contained plane tickets to Hawaii and a letter of invitation to serve on our newly-established Board of Directors. There was much rejoicing and talk of snorkeling, mountain climbing and jungle adventures at the Christmas dinner table. We went from "Joy to the World" to "Puff the Magic Dragon" and "Yellow Submarine" in nothing flat. David and I tried hard to cut through the conviviality to impress upon our beloved how this was not all a joke. We were now *business people* and their help was hereby being solicited.

Marshall, our oldest, quickly became the new Board's spokesperson. "Mom, Dad, this may not be as cool as being invited to all those White House Christmas parties when we lived in Washington, but it's very cool. We're all with you on this one."

So we had a buy-in, so to speak, on the Board idea. But looking back on the dynamics of those first several years, it's important to confess that despite our modest successes, we were constantly worried about money. Constantly. We used most of the proceeds from the sale of our home in Silver Spring to procure the mortgage for the B&B, saving some -- but not nearly enough -- out for what we correctly imagined would be a long and growing list of projects and essential purchases.

At the end of our first season, we were unduly optimistic. We had more money in the bank than we could ever have imagined. I don't remember what the total was exactly, but it made us feel like we could afford to go around the world, do all the projects and pay for another sapphire if we had to.

Alas, we did not take into account how we would live through the off-season. When the plays stopped playing at the end of October, our income plummeted to zero. How would we pay our mortgage? The utility bills? Food for us? The endless line of workmen knocking on our door to fulfill our dream of a new kitchen and many other improvements? Guests would not return until February!

Fortunately -- no, it has to have been more fortuitous than fortunate -- we had not given up our reporting jobs for AARP, so that was a modest income. And not long after we arrived, we turned 62, so quickly claimed our Social Security (early), providing a further -- albeit thin -- cushion. And truly fortuitously, David was asked to be a member of a World Bank consulting team working overseas for a month. To say the very least, it didn't take us long to discover that owning a B&B was complex in every way, but particularly financially.

While the Board of Directors undertaking came early in our career as business people, the Chamber of Commerce was actually our first stop. Meeting and mingling with other people who undoubtedly had more business experience than we did would be instructive, we thought. As it turned out, from time to time they did have helpful seminars -- the most memorable for me was how to do Excel spread sheets, something I still haven't mastered. I share that fact even though I realize this could affect my credibility as a successful businessperson. That said, our chief financial officer, David, doesn't know Quickbooks either. He prefers a system just one up from the abacus.

But no workshops at the Chamber would ever help conquer our "To Do" list, which no matter how hard we worked, continued to be approximately nine furlongs in length, with additions being made on a way-too-regular basis. No one at the Wine and Cheese Meet and Greets did any poor mouthing about how hard it was to survive the off-season financially. I was especially good at middle-of-the-sleepless-night ideas and inspirations, which I'd scribble down on one of my bright-aqua post-it notes on my bedside table and then try to interpret in the morning.

One morning I was stumped. The scribbled note said, "Aimee!" What did it mean? Who could Aimee be? By lunchtime, the only Aimee I'd been able to think of was one of the best interns I'd ever had in Washington. *Ahhhh. Interns! In my past life, they were always the key to getting through a long To Do list.* In fact, the secret non-fossil fuel for Washington, DC is interns. But did interns even exist in Ashland? Internships in Washington are highly competitive positions, for both the applicant and the employer. I remember when I hired my first one, begrudgingly accepting her condition that "I refuse to be the official Xerox person in the office."

"Xeroxing is a fact of life here," I said. "We all do it at one point or another."

"I didn't go to graduate school to collate copies," she said.

"Here's the thing," I finally said, "This is a big office with lots of assignments that do not require an advanced degree and if you don't want to Xerox, how would you like to answer the phone?"

It turned out she had a special talent for the phone, but she soon tired of that. When she asked for other assignments, I gave her some Xeroxing to do.

I decided to begin my quest for an intern when I returned from lunch at the Rotary Club, a service organization to which I've belonged for years. The memory of how well our highly-educated telephone operator performed lingered sweetly.

Often thought of as a social club for old business codgers, Rotary is actually one of the most vibrant forces for peace in the world. It provides more financial assistance and service to local communities throughout the world than all government assistance put together. I've been a Rotarian since I lived and worked in Belize in the early Nineties, not only because I believe in its tenets, but also because it enables me to meet people I otherwise wouldn't -- no matter where I am. *That day turned out to be particularly propitious.*

Looking around for a seat in the cavernous church hall where we Rotarians meet, I found a seat next to someone whom I didn't know who was attending for the first time. After the Pledge of Allegiance and the opening song -- there's a strict order to each week's agenda -- I introduced myself to the youngish brown-haired woman named Sue sitting next to me.

Eyeballing my large blue badge with my name and occupation on it, she said, "Looks like we're sort of in the same line of work. I'm the Dean of the School of Hotel and Hospitality at SOU (our local university). And it looks like you're in the hospitality business!"

Really, no kidding. Random seating and this is where I landed? It had to be quantum physics or something.

"Do you have any sort of an internship program for your students?" I said, skipping polite preliminaries, the words scrambling to get out of my mouth. "We're new in the B&B business and could really use some help." In my mind, I was already drawing up a position description for a lifesaving intern.

"Sure we do," she said. "We're always looking for placements locally. In fact this week is when we're doing the matching up between people who've requested them and our students. Send me an email describing what you're looking for. Here's my card."

"How great. I'll do it as soon as I get home. Thank you!"

Late that afternoon, our first intern of the dozen or so we've had over the years crossed the threshold, having been dispatched by my new friend, the Dean of Hospitality. This was clearly a benefit of living in a small town that things could happen so fast. Tall and blonde, Robin from Yamhill, Oregon didn't wait for me to describe the job as I envisioned it. After shaking my hand firmly (a requirement for working for us), she said, "I just want you to know Mrs. Runkel that I'll do *anything* that needs doing. Toilets. Spreadsheets. Gardening. Anything."

"We really, really, definitely, definitely need you. How would you feel about researching reservation software for us? We've got to move from all these tiny little pieces of paper stuck in the notebook (which constituted the system we inherited from the former owner) to something a lot more reliable. Here, you can sit right here."

I got up from my rickety rolling chair and motioned for her to sit down. "We're both left handed, but it's okay if you move the mouse to the right side."

"I think I can do that. We were actually just talking about reservation systems in class this morning. I know there are several different ones out there."

"We'll talk about your hours and your job description later, okay?" I said. "Don't worry, you'll get lots of hands-on experience here."

The website was the next big hurdle. Daughter Lucy's good friend Rachel offered to design one for us, as a volunteer. A near-daughter of ours, Rachel is one of those people who can do most anything she sets out to. Since it was now winter and we were in the zero income part of the year, her price was one we could afford and she a person whom we trusted. This was 2002, very early in the days of websites for Inns. A survey of other inns' websites proved disheartening and just plain uninspiring. The pictured rooms looked like they came from Designer's Workbook and had cinnamon-ginger-clove potpourri burbling on the side; the writing so saccharine it was diabetic. Any warts or tired bananas (doesn't everyone have one or two?) had obviously been airbrushed out. The rate schedules and

guidelines could have been written by a strict elementary school principal
-- no pets, no smoking, no children, no refunds, no exceptions. So many
things weren't allowed that you began to wonder if it would be all right to
snore or chew or fart, much less have seconds at breakfast.

The very same website (www.ashlandbandb.com) that went up in 2003
is still up today, only slightly modified. We were determined to have a website that was a true reflection of who we were and how we planned to operate. David and I wrote all the copy and put a picture of ourselves right up
there, as well as one of our resident chocolate lab.

Bring your dogs. We don't take deposits (this policy a result of neither
of us having figured out how to track them on the aforementioned spread
sheet). We have cotton sheets and we hang them outside (another picture).
We buy mostly local and organic (the 'green' market was just developing).
We like children very much and are happy to have them as guests. We
serve a full English tea in the afternoon. We poured as much charm as
tea, intent on letting people know not just what the Inn looked like and a
plate of breakfast had on it, but just exactly who their hosts would be. The
personal approach.

Of our fellow innkeepers, I think we may be the only ones who took this
approach to our website, but it's one we've never regretted. This is a business that couldn't be more personal, so we figured it best to begin developing the relationship before they ever got here. Our website still doesn't have
butterflies flying around or videos of people eating breakfast or drinking
wine on the patio next to award-winning blooming roses whilst chomping
on genetically-modified strawberries to the tune of Brahms. But it does
have our Certificate of Excellence from Trip Advisor, a picture of Hattie the
dog on the sofa and hidden red glass hearts in every room. (If a guest finds
theirs, they get a piece of local chocolate.)

This experience was but a needle in the haystack of other major items
on the "To Do" list. The inside of the house needed to be painted. We
needed to improve the kitchen (which was the same one put in when the

house was built in 1908). A payroll system was a must. New 100% cotton linens should be bought during winter sales. The stove was on its last legs. The garden needed a complete overhaul. The powder room needed to be finished -- the former owner had recommended that the live wires weren't a good thing to have with water or guests around. Electrocution of guests while doing their important business wouldn't be good for reviews. In what we should have realized was a hint, this bathroom project had been abandoned due to lack of funds just after the wires were wired. The former owner cautioned us and staff to be careful if we used it. We thought this might be above and beyond the call -- any call.

If our estimates were right, we needed at least $50,000 dollars, a lot more than we had in our back pockets after we saved out for the mortgage.

We'd already found that banks were and remained wary of loaning to B&Bs. The ones we talked to didn't consider us a real business. Plus, they asked for Profit and Loss statements before we even knew how to make one. We diagnosed ourselves with terminal angst. Whatever were we going to do? What the hell had we gotten ourselves into? We'd had to do lots of renovating in our past, but now our business depended on our ability to do it! Sleep became a commodity in short supply.

"We need to get lucky," I said to David. "Maybe someone rich will die and leave us money."

"Deedie! Get serious. We're in business now. Luck may be part of it, but dead relatives are not reliable funders and you know that," he said.

"I was just trying for some humor. Maybe there's a local bank that wants to invest in our fledgling effort."

"Maybe there is. I'm going to the Y. You're going to stay here for check-ins, right?" he said.

"Yup. We only have one check-in and I'll be here. Don't worry. I'll get serious."

He turned to go, then leaned over to give me a kiss. "I guess we should have thought of this before we came," he said resignedly.

I got up and wandered out to the garden, worn out psychically and physically. The late-afternoon sun burnt right through my blouse. I was still getting used to the fact that the most sizzling period of the day here was 5:00, quite unlike the East Coast. Looking around, all I could see were the flowers that needed to be dead-headed. And the boxwood needed to be trimmed. And the petunias needed water. Too tired to face it, I plopped down in the recliner chair under the canopy, succumbing to a day that had begun at 5:30 in the morning. When I was almost asleep, the gate from the parking lot slammed shut, causing me to leap up so awkwardly I fell down on the gravel, practically knocking over the chair as I did. As I got up from hands and knees, I ran my hand through my perspiration-laden hair and wished I'd remembered to put some lipstick on for check-in time.

"Welcome, welcome," I said. "So glad you're here," I said to the man and woman perched at the top of the steps. I could feel blood dribbling down my leg from the knee that took the hit when I rolled out of the recliner.

"Are you okay? So sorry to disturb you," the gentleman guest called down, looking toward my bloody knee. He wore a hazelnut-colored suit, with quite a nice lime green silk tie to match. His wife wore patent leather heels and a tailored apricot linen dress like I used to wear to the office in Washington -- both a distinct departure from Ashland's casual dress code. I couldn't remember where they were from.

"Oh, I'm fine, thanks," I said, brushing the gravel from my scraped hands. "Help me remember where you're from. Is it Ken? And??? I know I should know, but my brain's on overload this afternoon."

"We are actually only from Medford -- we bid on your donation of a free night at the University Foundation Auction and won! I'm Ken and this is my wife Lindsey. What a beautiful setting." Medford's the big city (Population 60,000 vs 20,000) eleven miles down the road and where we shop for the things we buy wholesale or at the big-box stores. Sometimes we call it Dreadford because its cultural factor compared to Ashland's is dreadful (which is a dreadfully snobbish thing to say).

"Thanks so much. C'mon in and let me show you around. We're in our rookie year of being innkeepers and all we see at this point is what all needs to be done."

"That sounds like about par for the course for a new business," Ken said.

As we moved through the Inn, I pointed to all the visible items on the Project List. The kitchen. The painting. The garden.

"You must have a friendly banker," Ken said.

Before I could answer, Lindsey said, "Ken's a banker himself."

"Oh really?" I said. "Then you probably know how difficult it is for B&B's to find financing for mortgages and upgrades."

"Actually, I don't know that," Ken said. By now we were sitting in the living room drinking homemade lemonade. "You'll have to tell me more about that in the morning. Right now, we've got to unpack and get off to dinner and the theatre."

"'Sounds good. We're so glad you were the high bidders," I said, standing up.

Ken patted my shoulder and said, "And we're glad, new as you are, that you saw fit to donate to the Foundation. That sort of gesture is good business, but you already know that."

Ken and Lindsey retreated to their room while I cleared up from tea and prepped the kitchen for the next morning. Little did Ken and Lindsey know all we *didn't* know; but with them under our roof, they'd have first-hand experience of what things we did do well before they left. I couldn't wait to tell David, even though I was consumed with guilt about telling guests everything that was wrong with the inn. Blurting has always been my long suit.

"Believe it or not, our check-in's a local banker," I said walking swiftly through our condo to the back patio where he was planted with a post-Y gin and tonic and *The New York Times*.

"What? How could he be a local banker?"

"Because he lives in Medford and bid on the night here we donated to the University Foundation," I said. "I'm really excited about this."

"What bank? What's his position?" David said, picking up his newspaper again.

"The truth is, I don't know," I said. "But let me Google him. I'll find out. Maybe he'll be so impressed he'll lend us all the money we need," I said. "I'm having a glass of wine and beginning to hope really hard," I said, going into the house. David had returned to *The New York Times*, engrossed.

"Red or white?" he muttered.

Our season over, we were deep into planning for each of the projects on the list.

Our banker guest -- now friend -- had turned out to be the *president* and founder of a Medford bank who offered to lend us money before we ever even got up our nerve to ask! Since the bank would soon be opening a branch in Ashland, Anne Hathaway's would be a good foothold, as he called it. Before we signed the final papers, we consulted the accounting firm we'd been directed to.

"Should we be worried about too much debt?" we asked.

"Debt is good," came the answer.

That's a good thing, because we're in a lot of debt right now, I thought. *A lot of debt. Daunting debt. We were paying out thousands of dollars a month. Could we, would we be able to sustain this? Were we in our right minds?*

I Googled "Debt vs Income ratios," and any other economic platitude I could find that would make me feel more confident. I resisted the temptation to consult Allen Greenspan or David's contacts at the World Bank. Instead, we were ready to nominate Ken for Banker of the Year for having given us the impression (and the checks) to make us think we knew what we were doing and that our Debt to Income ratio was just fine.

From practically the very beginning, whenever we were full (an increasingly frequent occurrence) and couldn't take a reservation, we referred guests to the Travelers' Accommodations caddy-corner across the street. Sweet little cottages built at the end of the 19th century, they were popular because they had kitchenettes, Jacuzzis, nice porches and gardens. When they came on the market, we couldn't help thinking they would be a great asset to our business, seven more rooms for our growing number of guests. But we couldn't fathom how we'd pay for them.

We felt we really couldn't afford more debt, so we tried to think of other sources of a down payment, having figured out that the income would more than pay for the expenses. Our modest Federal retirement accounts, though, would make a great down payment. But was this the right thing to do? Was this a smart move? This would make us one of the biggest B&Bs in town and mean we'd have to expand our staff, among many, many other things. And also leave two people in their sixties with not much of a retirement cushion.

One is not supposed to talk business at Rotary Club. Its founder, Paul Harris, felt hard-working business people should devote this weekly occasion to solely to fellowship and service. Once again, I boldly violated this rule by purposely sitting next to the innkeeper in town with several more rooms than we'd have if we expanded.

"Michael," I said, "How did you and Laurie make the decision to add more rooms when you first got into the business?"

"Deedie," he said, "Easy." He took out his pen and pulled a napkin down between us, on which he wrote, "Rooms = $$."

"Hmm. That makes sense," I said. "And really helps. Thanks so much."

"Now we better be careful or we'll get caught talking business," he said, patting me on the shoulder. We stood up to sing "God Bless America" and pledge allegiance to the flag. Sitting down again, I turned to the person on my left, one of the many financial advisors in town.

"Say, would you mind helping me with a hypothetical?" I said. "I'm trying to weigh whether real estate in Ashland is as good -- or better -- an investment as the market, as in my Federal retirement fund. You willing to offer an off-the-cuff, against the rules of the club, opinion."

"Easy, Deedie," he said. "Look at the Chamber of Commerce's newsletter. You'll see -- real estate in Ashland is flourishing, unlike the market."

The purchase of the cottages brought our room total up to fourteen. Friends accused us of becoming real estate moguls, turning our blocks of East Main Street into East Runkel Street. Scaling up turned out to be just as easy as we thought it would, but definitely meant we were not the "Ma and Pa" business we were in the beginning.

When we told our kids of our acquisition, they immediately wanted to know when the next Board of Directors meeting was. Whoops. We'd forgotten to tell them we'd been advised by our business lawyer that a business this size, while it wasn't that large, would probably end up being a liability for the kids and they probably didn't want to assume all or any of the liability we had.

"No more Hawaii?" Lucy said. "We really loved those Profit and Loss statements."

"You guys will always be part of Anne Hathaway's and you can see our P&L statements any time you want to. But no official responsibilities," David said.

"We'll be official tasters," Marshall said. "We're good at that. And by the way, whatever are you going to do with those huckleberries I saw in the kitchen?"

Huckleberry Baby

Put an iron skillet in the freezer the night before.

Preheat oven to 450.

Add to blender:

- 2 C. milk

- 2 C. flour

- 4 eggs

- 1 tsp. vanilla

- Dash of salt

1. Blend thoroughly and let sit for 10 minutes.

2. Rub softened butter on frozen skillet thickly, taking care not to miss a spot.

3. Pour in liquid.

4. Add 11/2 C. huckleberries to middle of liquid. Swirl a little.

5. Cook for 20-25 minutes.

6. Serve immediately, before it falls. This is actually a huge popover, or a berry Yorkshire pudding.

7. Serve with maple syrup or buttermilk syrup.

Small Worlds — Three
Percent for Six Percent

We just moved to Oragon [sic] and my parents brought me here.
Marigold, 7/06

"Do you give discounts?" some potential guests ask us.

For the first few years, the answer was, "No." I was determined that not a single guest would feel as I always do about the person sitting next to me on an airplane -- *they probably got a better deal than I did.* We said nope to AARP and again to AAA.

Then one winter, it dawned on us that discounts could be fun. They wouldn't have to be for a lot of money and they could stand for something -- something we believed in -- say, teachers, or Peace Corps or Rotary. Or maybe it could be something about us -- our University, our high schools. (While we'd never considered ourselves particularly fascinating, one thing we discovered as innkeepers is how fascinating our guests think we are.)

"What do you think about chocolate lab owners?" I asked.

David thought we already heard enough about dogs at the breakfast table.

"What about Adult Children of Alcoholics," I asked. See how many would ask for *that* discount. Now I was laughing. We were both laughing. If you're a typewriter eater of corn on the cob. If you still drive a stick shift. If you have more than five children. If you don't wear a bra.

By the end of the evening, we had a list we were ready to load into the handsome maroon leatherette information notebooks we put in each room. These included an overabundance of information about the Inn, What to Expect, Where to Eat Dinner, The Provenance of the Art in the House and now the newest category -- **Discounts**.

Initially, these discounts made guests skeptical. No one had ever stayed at an establishment with such a list:

- Born in 1941 (like us)

- Graduates of Radnor or Cochranton, Pa. High Schools (ours)

- Graduates of Penn State (where we met)

- Returned Peace Corps Volunteers or staff or parents of volunteers (I was staff, we were parents of)

- Members of the American Contract Bridge League (David)

- Rotarian (me)

- Left-handed (both of us) ….

- Friends (as in Quakers)

- Family and Friends of Family (FOF)

There was no double-dipping nor were trifectas permitted for these discounts, but they attracted attention.

Revealing that list had an unexpected benefit: it skipped the "Do you Know?" phase and told people exactly who we were. One Thursday afternoon I'd checked in a foursome of first-timers. The women were sisters and the one who lived in Oregon had made the reservation, so her name was the only one we had. I told them to be sure to read those notebooks in their rooms – they contained everything they could possibly want to know about the Inn, the town and us.

A short time later, as I was busy putting out tea in the dining room, one of the men from the group asked if I had a minute to chat. "I've completed the assignment you gave us and am ready for the quiz," he said.

Eventually I discovered that he had read the notebook, as I told him to, and knew enough now to take a test on it.

"I just want to know how much of a discount I get if I went to Lower Merion High School?" he asked.

"*Lower Merion?* You have to pay *double* if you went to Lower Merion," I said.

Lower Merion was my high school's archrival in all sports, reputedly the oldest school rivalry in the country. I looked up at him and beamed, proud of my quick comeback. "I'm afraid I didn't catch your name when you first came – we had your reservation under your sister-in-law – so what's your name and where did you live?" I asked.

"My name is Peter Jones, and admittedly I only went to Lower Merion for one year," he said.

Feeling cheekier than usual, I said, "Ah, I bet you transferred to some fancy place like Episcopal Academy."

"Huh?" he said. "How would you know a fact like that?" He folded his arms across the chest of his bright yellow LaCoste shirt. It had been a while since I'd seen an "alligator" shirt.

"I just guessed. We Radnor girls used to date boys from Episcopal every now and then."

"I know that's true because I dated a girl from Radnor. A very beautiful girl. You wouldn't know her because I'm much older than you are. Nettie Beeson. I still remember her well," he said.

"Nettie Beeson? She's my sister! Now I remember you, Peter Jones. *Pete* Jones, I can't believe it. Neither will Nettie. I am the *little* sister, so I don't really remember anything about you except your name."

"Does this mean we now qualify for the *Family* discount?" Pete Jones asked.

"No way, Pete Jones. You had your chance to get into the family a long time ago. I'm calling Nettie right now to tell her that the lost has been found," I said, smiling and hoping he'd be as amused as I was with myself.

Our prior lives inside the beltway continue to be a rich source of small worldisms.

Back stories have become front stories, sometimes revealing inner, some might say intimate, workings of our careers not previously public.

"You worked at the Justice Department under Thornburgh?" a lawyer guest asked David one morning when the chat was about what to do as a business to comply with the Americans with Disabilities act. It was a centerpiece of Thornburgh's legacy, and David had played a big role in its passage and was present for its signing.

Sitting at the other end of the table, I cringed a little, wondering if our guests would worry about staying in a *Republican* B&B. Yes, David had worked as Director of Communications for Attorney General Dick Thornburgh in President George H.W. Bush's Administration. Our guests are primarily Democrats, like me; so I always worry a little when it becomes clear that ours is what I call a "mixed" marriage.

"Our son was in the Criminal Division then. Maybe you knew him?" the guest asked. Jon Sebring?

"Oh, of course I knew him. He was a great guy. What's he doing now?" David asked.

The father beamed, as I heaved a sigh of relief. "He's with Williams and Connolly. Doing quite well, we think. He'll be tickled that we found you all the way out here in Oregon."

While we don't bring up our Washington pasts often -- focusing instead on our guests and the plays they are seeing -- there in fact are several pictures of our family members and ourselves with Presidents on the fruit-covered walls of the Powder Room off the dining room. Once discovered by each group of guests, it becomes a destination. The gallery includes:

- Our son, daughter-in-law and their baby with President Clinton. Our son is a political organizer in Portland and the President was belatedly trying (unsuccessfully) to entice him to work on Hillary's campaign in 2008 for $100 a week and a bathroom photo.

- David and me with President George H.W. Bush and Mrs. Bush at the annual Christmas party, when David was at Justice and I held the same job at Peace Corps. Mrs. Bush greeted us as "Peace and Justice."

- Our daughter and son-in-law with a very realistic-looking cut-out of President Obama on Inauguration night in San Francisco, where nearly $10,000 was raised for community works.

So the six degrees of separation theory has become as accepted as e=mc2 at Anne Hathaway's. We've accumulated nearly as many coincidences as we have new friends. In addition to David's former colleague, that particular day our breakfast table featured the chance encounter of a midwife with a child she'd delivered 30-odd years earlier on Mercer Island, Washington. In the same week, long-lost Delta Gamma sorority sisters from the University of Michigan found each other across the cheese soufflés.

One Friday, the breakfast entrée was a Community Supported Agriculture (CSA) Frittata, using as many ingredients as possible from the weekly box we get as our share delivered by the local Fry Family Farm.

We were in the kitchen. David was trying to decide between the baby squash and the chard. He's always in charge of the big egg dishes since I hate eggs and believe it or not have never eaten a one of them in over seventy-five years.

"What are we going to do with all this cabbage?" David asked. Once August rolls around, the heads of cabbage seem to proliferate in the box. Purple. White. Yellowish. Cabbage galore.

"Maybe you could put some in the frittata," I said, only half serious.

Cabbage always reminds me of my first trip to Africa as a Peace Corps staffer. I spent ten days with a volunteer who had convinced the women in her village to grow cabbage galore. I'd never seen so much cabbage. I don't think I'd ever seen it growing, actually.

"By the way," he said, "That young couple with the little boy is coming over from the cottages for breakfast," David said, beginning to crack the first of the fourteen eggs. "Her name is Joyce. She thinks she knows you."

At that moment, the door from the dining room opened and Joyce poked her head in.

"I hope you remembered we were coming for breakfast today," she said.

"Yup. We have you in the count," I said. "You look *so, so* familiar. Do we know each other?"

"I don't think so. I'm afraid I don't even know your name yet. But I have to tell you, this is the perfect way to de-compress after defending my dissertation," she said. "We're having a great time." She closed the door gently. I went back to arranging fruit artfully for the first course. Fruit art is what we call it. *Who's Joyce?*

Ten minutes later, I went into the dining room to announce breakfast. "Time for the breakfast march." I called. "C'mon, breakfast clubbers," I said, leading the way to the garden.

Older guests are always surprised to find I know about the old radio show, *Don McNeil's Breakfast Club,* which is where I got the line. My Granny was a regular at Don McNeil's table, a wildly popular radio show that ran for close to 40 years beginning in the Thirties. When I stayed home sick, Granny and I would listen together.

"It's random, free-range sitting," I announced as we arrived in the garden where four tables were carefully set. I noticed that Joyce, the newly-minted PhD, and her family was sitting with long-time guests, Bryan and Marilyn.

After the fruit course, David came out with the freshly-baked frittata, and began explaining about Community Supported Agriculture and our farmer and how we just throw as much of whatever's in the box into the frittata and it was all inspired by our daughters Lucy and Sara.

"I wanted to put some cabbage in too, but David wouldn't let me," I said.

As I walked back into the kitchen with the empty coffee jug, I overheard Joyce telling Bryan she knows all about CSAs. They get one in Eugene.

When I returned, she and Bryan were comparing the rigors of researching and writing a dissertation. "Mine involved several trips back to Africa, where I served as a Peace Corps volunteer," I heard her say.

Marilyn broke in immediately. "You have to talk about *that* with Deedie. She worked at Peace Corps. Did you realize you get a discount for being a volunteer?"

As I pulled up my chair, I heard Joyce say. "In Senegal. A really remote part of the country. I worked with women and their gardens, actually."

"Joyce, JOYCE. It's you. Now I know who you are," I said. "You grew a lot – *a very lot* – of cabbage with those women did you?" I couldn't believe it. This was the same Joyce I lived with for a week, the same volunteer who sent soil back to Washington, DC from Senegal to her father who worked for the Soil Service. He researched what would be best to grow in the soil there and told his daughter it was cabbage. Joyce then convinced the women in her village to grow cabbage with the seeds her dad donated.

By the time I got there, a cabbage crisis was in full force. The women were very proud of it. They'd stack it carefully and artfully in the marketplace twice a week, but no one bought any. No one knew what to do with it. People in that part of the world had never seen a cabbage, didn't know what to do with cabbage. *No wonder Joyce looked familiar.*

I ran around to Joyce's chair. She stood up and we gave each other a long hug. Tears washed down my cheeks. The children bringing us mangoes, sweeping the dirt floor of her hut three times a day, the endless rows of cabbage the women were so proud of but wouldn't eat, the village baby who died at birth, the dancing and drumming, my inability to eat with my right hand, as required -- I was back in Senegal, just that quick. It was my first official trip overseas from headquarters. I'd added on some leave so I could really get the feel of what it meant to be a volunteer.

Now it was Joyce's turn to talk. "Yup. We sure did grow cabbages. Deedie was right there and saw them all. We tried cooking some, but no one would even try it. We even tried disguising it as a peanut-based dish, to no avail. And I don't think I ever thanked you enough, Deedie, for all those other recipes you sent me. Unfortunately, I was never successful in getting people to eat all it. None of it, to tell you the truth."

"I sure know at least a little how they felt – and you felt – now that I get the CSA box," I said. "We always have cabbage left over. I put it in the compost and hope it does amazing things for the soil. And I think of your cabbage crop when I do it. Now, what did you do your thesis on?"

"*The African Woman Farmer and her Choice of Crops,*" she said.

The rest of the guests clapped. Marilyn nudged Joyce and said, "Be sure you get your discount when you check out."

Later that month, another new story walked through the door.

Marlene was celebrating her retirement as News Director of NBC San Francisco and was very excited to hear we were from Washington. Her long news career had started in Pierre, South Dakota and gotten a big boost when, with information from her intern, she broke a national story from Washington.

"I never worked in DC myself, but a young summer intern I sent there discovered our state's Congressman had secretly divorced his wife, also from South Dakota, and married a beauty queen. By reading the *real estate transfers* in the *Washington Post*. That's six-point type he had to read! I was so proud of him, and of myself for telling him he should read everything he could lay his hands on and one day he'd find some buried news. We broke that story, which was a big one for our small state."

"Huh," David said. "Congratulations! We know Tom Daschle very slightly, but Deedie worked with his first wife and is still friends with her. Wait 'til she hears this story." I was sitting at the desk in the office while she and David talked in the foyer and couldn't help overhearing the conversation. I certainly did know his former wife, the one left with three small children. She was my friend and colleague. We worked together everyday. And schemed about how we could get the news of such scandalous behavior out with no fingerprints. "You're kidding," I said, running into the hallway. "YOU broke that story. I can't believe it. Our office was always blamed for being the source and it was your intern after all! The Congressman himself actually accused me over the phone for being the leaker of the information." David patted me on the shoulder, a sign that maybe I'd over-reacted.

I excused myself immediately. This was information, albeit 20 years later, that my friend, the ex-wife -- who happened to then work at the aforementioned Williams and Connolly law firm -- needed to know. Our final and official exoneration right here at Anne Hathaway's B&B. "Listen," I said. "You're not going to believe this, honestly…" I started off the message on her voicemail. David quietly closed the door of the office, with a wave and a smile.

Our quirky discounts also had the unforeseen effect of attracting a younger crowd. One day I answered a call from Grace, a young Friend (Quaker) from Chicago who said she'd heard about us from her parents, who saw our advertisement in *Friends Journal*. She'd gone to our website and loved the discounts.

"We're coming to Oregon for a friend's wedding and for the theatre and wondered if you had space and what the discount was," she asked.

When Grace and her husband came, we discovered we had more than faith in common. "I noticed your name is Runkel and I have to ask you something," she said. "When I was eleven, I went to this tiny music camp in Ohio and there was a girl there named Sara Runkel. Is she related, by any small chance?" she asked.

"Yes, Sara Runkel is our daughter," I said. Remembering how unhappy Sara had been at camp and still feeling a little guilty about her bad experience, I asked, "How did you get to know her?" Sara was there during her most withdrawn and monosyllabic pubescent years and my impression had been that she kept herself pretty isolated at camp.

"The first night of camp I was in the dining room, feeling miserable," Grace said. "I might have even been crying. My parents had just dropped me off in the middle of nowhere and I had no idea what to do. I'd never been to camp before and didn't even know how to get a dinner tray. Everyone was standing up singing some song I didn't know and that made it even harder. That's when I found Sara. I think she might have been crying also because she had big red blotches on her face and chest. She was sort of hanging around. I got up all my nerve and asked her if she was new like me. Then I told her about how my parents had just dumped me there and I didn't even know how we were supposed to eat."

"What did she say?" I asked, dreading the answer.

Sara had told her story straight. *Her* parents had dropped her at the airport in Belize City, Central America, she'd flown to Miami, had to change terminals from one end of the airport to the other and from there flew to Pittsburgh, Pa. and then some people she hardly knew picked her up and drove her to camp, dropping her off in the driveway.

"I couldn't believe it. I'd never heard of Belize, but it sounded far away. When I heard *that*, I didn't feel so bad. We gave each other hugs and were friends for all of camp and then I lost touch with her," she said.

That night, I related the conversation to David at dinner.

"I think we can say unequivocally that the discounts are working," he said. "Have you called Sara yet?"

Anne Hathaway's CSA Frittata

Polenta:
- 1 C. corn meal
- 2 C. water, added slowly whisking.
- 1 t. salt

Cook until it softly boils for 5 minutes, stirring all the time. Add ½ c. salsa, or any other spicy, tasty thing that's languishing in your 'fridge. Put in loaf pan overnight, covered with saran.

Filling:
Saute all fresh ingredients: garlic, onion, zucchini, carrots, kale, chard, basil, parsley, eggplant until pretty thoroughly cooked.

Assembly:
1. Slice polenta thinly and put on hot griddle until it acquires crust on both sides.
2. Spray 9x13 pan lightly. Line with polenta slices.
3. Place layer of filling.
4. Sprinkle with parmesan.
5. Repeat process
6. Garnish top with pepper slices.
7. Pour 14 eggs beaten lightly over the vegetables.

Cook at 425 for about 25 minutes until golden brown.
* CSA stands for Community Supported Agriculture. We buy a share of a local farmer's produce for the season, in return for which we receive a box of fresh produce each week. The contents of the strata are dependent on what's in the box!

Divine Intervention

The McClouds were right out of central casting for weary clergy people. The Reverend wore a tie, maybe it was a clip-on, a slightly rumpled white shirt and a dark suit made shiny as his black shoes from multiple dry-cleanings. He and his bride were about the same height, rather slight in stature. Mrs. McCloud, which is how she was introduced, had a pale white dress with lavender flowers scattered all over it, buttons down the front and a matching cloth belt. With the temperature in the mid-nineties, seeing that she was wearing stockings with her low-heeled pristinely polished white shoes made me feel hotter than I already was. I was relieved for her that she wasn't wearing the white gloves I bet she did most Sundays.

She reminded me of Miss Molly Obdyke from my days as a Presbyterian Sunday School girl. Totally proper, prim and pristinely clean. They seemed to have brought a time machine along, perhaps inside the ancient black leather suitcase Rev. McCloud left just outside the office door. It dialed me back to the Fifties. I tried to imagine them joining others walking down the streets of Ashland, where the Birkenstocks or sneakers, shorts and tee shirts abound.

The McClouds' visit was completely unplanned, on their part. The secretary at Easterly Christian Heritage Fellowship Church had called the day before to ask if we possibly had a room for Sunday night. Leaders of the congregation had decided their pastor was on the edge of ministerial burnout and needed to get away. *And* it was their wedding anniversary.

I'd just checked out veteran guests, the Maxwells, a day early because their dog was ill, which meant we indeed did have a room available.

"Our pastor is just so worn out, we're all worried that he's going to quit or get sick. He hasn't taken even a day's vacation in more than a year. You know how it is with pastors – theirs is a 24/7 job. We've heard it's really nice in Ashland and I chose your place because Mrs. McCloud's name is also Anne with an 'e' just like yours. I thought that might make her more receptive to coming," Muriel the secretary explained.

"You mean *tomorrow?*" I asked.

"Yes, and here's the thing – we're going to surprise him with this gift at Sunday's church service. We have no idea whether or not he'll accept, but we thought we ought to have reservations for them somewhere. It's important they have a destination, don't you think? We'll pay in advance. And you do serve breakfast, right? We don't want them to have to spend very much of their own money. The fact of the matter is they don't have very much money," she said under her breath. "Doing the Lord's work is hard, you know. It's so important that he get some rest."

Remembering my lengthy conversation with Muriel made me feel as if I knew the McClouds already. I couldn't tell if their drooping shoulders were a sign of weariness or age, but they were both quite present and curious.

"We've never stayed in a bed and breakfast before," the pastor said haltingly, "So I guess you're going to have to tell us what to do next!" He smiled broadly.

"Oh of course," I interjected. "We give all of our guests an orientation and a map so you can get around town easily."

"We've never even been to Ashland," he said apologetically. "We're both from Kansas originally."

"Well, come with me and I'll show you to your room," David said.

"Can we wander a bit first?" Anne McCloud asked.

Soon they were both busy scanning the living room and the floor-to-ceiling book shelves. "What a lot of books," Rev. McCloud noted. "I could stay here all day. Look at this, Anne, they even have an old Bible. Bless me, I don't think I've ever seen one this big or so old," he said, stooping down to look at its weary gold and green back more closely.

"It's a family Bible from my grandmother's side. There are all kinds of events recorded in it," I said, lifting it out from the shelf and putting it on the dining room table.

"Really. This place is so much like *my* grandmother's, I can almost smell the rhubarb pie cooking in her oven," Mrs. McCloud said.

As they left with David to go to their room, they were both chatting back and forth about old bibles and rhubarb.

That morning as we manufactured yet another breakfast in the kitchen, we had talked about the McClouds' impending arrival. Would they want to go to the theatre? Why didn't I ask that when I was talking to Muriel? What denomination minister was he? Where exactly was Easterly? Wasn't it funny a minister lived in a town called *Easterly*? Whoops, I forgot to ask if they had any dietary restrictions.

"This will be fun if it happens," David said. "He sounds like my mother's minister – hard working and tireless."

"I agree. We just have to make sure they feel comfortable."

The call from Muriel came just at noon.

"They're coming! They're coming. We've just told the McClouds about our surprise plan and they've gone home to pack," she said excitedly.

"How wonderful," I said. "We'll be ready for them when they arrive here. Do they know the way?"

"Oh yes. I printed out the directions and everything and put it in the envelope we gave him at the end of the service. I even put a bow around it. He was SO surprised. And can you believe it, it's their wedding anniversary?

Mrs. McCloud actually started to cry. She said that nothing like this had ever happened to them before in more than 40 years of marriage!"

"That's just great. We'll be ready for them and guide them through how to have a good time in Ashland. That's our job."

"He's so tired, he might not want to do anything but sit on that front-porch swing outside their room that I saw on your website. Will they have to share that swing with other guests, by the way?"

"Nope. The swing's all theirs. Thank you so much, Muriel. We'll take good care of your pastor and make sure they both have a restful time."

"Thank you and good-bye, Anne."

"My name is actually Deedie...." Muriel had already cut off.

When I told the staff that Calla would be occupied by guests celebrating their anniversary, they got out some big white ribbon and tied a bow on the doorknob. David went to Safeway for some champagne to have in their room in a silver bucket, crystal flutes along side it. We weren't sure they would even be interested in an alcoholic drink, but decided the gesture was worth it.

"Are you sure it's wise to give them alcohol?" David said.

"We're going to go with our instincts," I responded, moving from the sink to the counter to give him a little kiss.

On our way home that evening, a vision of love appeared across the street from our condo. There were the McClouds on their front porch, sitting close together on the swing, each with a glass of champagne in their hand. He'd taken his jacket off, rolled up his sleeves and was barefoot. Later, they planned to go to the free outdoor show before the play at Oregon Shakespeare Festival, which David had recommended. They'd told him *Romeo and Juliet* tickets were way beyond their budget, even though they both agreed it would be the perfect thing to do on their anniversary. They shared that they'd both taught high school English before Mr. McCloud "got the call," and had always loved the play. David urged them to be on the look-out for people who might be trying to sell tickets cheaply that they couldn't use at the last minute. And off they went to the free outdoor Green Show, held every night adjacent to the theatres.

Having the McClouds as guests perked us both up after a long week of many guests, breakfasts and scheduling challenges. While they weren't our typical sophisticated guests from one of the cities to the North and South, they were genuine and open to making the absolute best of being in Ashland. I wished they *would* get to go to *Romeo and Juliet*. But maybe they'd just stay home and read the Bible, which was one alternative they'd come up with after David briefed them all there was "to do" in Ashland. We couldn't wait for breakfast the next morning to hear how their unexpected evening had unfolded.

"Don't you think we could sneak up to the box office and buy some tickets and then get someone to give them to the McClouds?" I asked David as we were fixing our dinner. "I really want them to go to the theatre."

"I know, I know. But like your instincts about the champagne, my instinct is we shouldn't. We're already giving them a discount, remember."

"Yup, it's the first -- and probably the last -- one we've ever given for doing the work of the Lord. Muriel the secretary asked for it. I'd never been asked, so I had to say 'yes.' How could you not?" I said.

We both agreed that breakfast was going to have its own drama with the McClouds on board. "I wonder how they'll blend with everyone else," I said.

"Deedie, they're professional blenders! That's part of doing the Lord's work," David said. "Let's take the dog for a walk on this nice evening."

The McClouds arrived early for breakfast. From the kitchen, we could hear them talking animatedly with other guests. Blending well, I thought to myself.

"I remember seeing *Romeo and Juliet* done by my high school in Kansas, but I could never have imagined ever seeing a production this large. It was just plain heavenly," the pastor said in a strong sermon voice we could hear clearly.

"Great," David said. "They *did* go."

"Sounds like it," I said, turning down NPR on the radio so I could overhear the conversation better. Alas, within minutes, everyone had moved into the garden, where the tables were set for breakfast, so I turned it back up.

When we went out to the garden after the last person was served breakfast, Anne and Clyde (which we'd overheard him introduce himself as) were beaming.

A very animated Anne McCloud was holding forth. How could she have changed so dramatically in less than 24 hours? When they checked in, she hung back, she seemed a little meek, said little. Now here she was regaling everyone at breakfast about seeing *Romeo and Juliet* the night before. Had she taken an Oprah pill? I couldn't help noticing she was wearing sneakers. At least she'd been somewhat Ashlandized.

"We really hadn't planned to go. The few tickets available cost more than our weekly groceries. So we were standing outside the Box Office deciding what to do and this man walks up to Clyde and asks if we'd like a pair of tickets. 'How much?' my husband asked. The answer was 'Nothing! Enjoy the show.' Can you imagine? When Clyde told him it was our anniversary, he said, 'Happy Anniversary' and walked off.

"Can you believe our seats were *in the fifth row!* Once we sat down, I was still in a state of total disbelief. That's when I saw this woman coming right toward me. I was sure she was coming to tell me there'd been a mistake, that these were actually her seats. She was stepping over everyone's feet carefully and trying not to crush this huge bouquet she was carrying." Breathless, Anne stopped for a moment and put her hand on Clyde's. "When she finally got to us, she asked me my name, introduced herself, and then explained that my seat had been her mother's seat for 31 years and her mom had died this past winter and she wanted to honor her mother by giving these flowers to whoever was sitting in her mother's seat. I began to cry a little and I admit it. The next thing I know, she's handing me that bouquet and telling me her mother's name was Ann without an 'e.'" Anne stopped to hunt for a hankie to deal with the copious tears flowing down her crimson cheeks.

Clyde reached over with a perfectly folded handkerchief to wipe Anne's tears away, and then sat back and lifted his glasses to wipe away his own.

"So my bride sat through this incredible performance with a bouquet much larger than the one she carried on our wedding day," Clyde said, in sermon voice, looking around at his breakfast congregation. "We decided as we went to sleep that some sort of divine intervention had occurred. We actually believe that," he said, to the flock of nodding heads around him.

Our minister for the day had a rapt audience of three tables in his thrall. Once he finished speaking, momentary, stunned silence reigned. Then long-time guest, Martin clapped, then another. Soon everyone began to clap. Anne and Clyde looked around, disbelieving. Then people stood up and kept on clapping. Anne and Clyde had their handkerchiefs out again. I teared up myself. One couple started to leave, but was stopped.

"But wait, there's more to the story," Anne said eagerly. "No one here knows just *how* perfect it was for us to see *Romeo and Juliet*."

Martin Magid looked over at her and said with a smile, "Were you a Capulet and Clyde a Montague?"

"Well, that's actually almost true," Clyde said definitively. "Our two families haven't gotten along for two generations – ever since her great aunt Clara married my great uncle Clyde, which is actually against the law. You may know, it's illegal in Kansas for first cousins to marry. And no one even acknowledges that God commanded many cousins to marry, including Zelophehad's five daughters, Eleazar's daughters and others. As for us, people just thought we were entirely too young."

"How interesting," I said. Others had begun talking. "Now how do you spell that Z-name? I don't think I've ever heard it."

"It really is interesting, isn't it," Anne said, as she passed the rhubarb marmalade to Clyde. "Taste this marmalade, dear. It's just like my grandmother's."

Our first standing ovation breakfast lasted nearly until check-out time. On my way to the office from the kitchen, I encountered Clyde and Anne in the living room taking pictures with a camera I didn't know anyone used anymore.

"Let's take one of you two," I said.

"Okay, Deedie. But don't show my tennis shoes," Anne requested.

"Be sure Muriel gets a copy. She was so excited."

In the office, Clyde scanned my hat collection, able to identify the provenance of nearly every single one on the wall.

"Now how do you know all those hats, *and* the Bible *and* Shakespeare and lots more that I don't even know about?" I asked.

"Deedie, let me tell you something. Doing the Lord's work requires one to wear many hats. It looks to me as if you and David wear as many as you have nailed to the wall. Thank you so much for everything. And I hope it's okay with you that we took the rest of the champagne with us so we can have some at home."

Rhubarb Marmalade

From a B&B near Ithaca, New York via the Liversidges

- 2 lemons
- 1 orange
- 8 cups diced rhubarb
- 6 cups sugar
- ¾ Cup chopped walnuts or raisins or pecans

1. In a food processor, chop the lemons and orange.
2. In a heavy saucepan, combine the chopped lemons and oranges, rhubarb and sugar.
3. Simmer over low heat for 45 minutes.
4. Add nuts and simmer 15 more minutes.

Place the marmalade in sterilized jars. Makes about 10 half pints

Salmon Benvolio

"Benvolio. David said we were having Benvolio for breakfast," my cousin Ginny said. "And we can't figure out what that might be. What *is* Benvolio?"

By this time my New Jersey relatives knew we often served up fanciful names at breakfast. David was at a bridge game and it was Cousins Night at the condo. We were sitting around the living room in our quarters, a block away from the Inn, enjoying the rare chance to share what we call "Backstage at the Inn" stories with visiting friends and relatives. Being able to relax under a different roof and drink a few glasses of wine is the ultimate for me. If I'm at the Inn, I'm prone to notice cobwebs, afraid I'll disturb guests, be tempted to answer emails or feel I have to answer the phone instead of letting the answering service do their job. In the condo, I don't give a damn about cobwebs unless we've invited someone for dinner. Cousins don't care, I'd decided.

Ginny poured herself a little more wine.

"Tonight at dinner we were all trying to think of what it might be. Italian? Is that right? We just couldn't figure out what it was." The cousins nodded in unison.

"I even worked in an Italian restaurant for years, and I never heard of *Benvolio*," Liz said. Even before Liz finished, I started to laugh.

"What's so funny?" Betsy asked.

85

"You guys saw *Romeo and Juliet* yesterday. Remember Benvolio, Romeo's friend? The one who tries to get Romeo's mind off Rosaline, before he met Juliet, and convince him there are lots of girls available?" I didn't want to laugh again for fear they'd think I was making fun of them. "We *know* him. He's coming for breakfast tomorrow morning. It's one of our traditions. We try to have an actor join us once or twice a week. We call it our Actors for Breakfast program."

This time they all laughed with me.

"Of course, I know who Benvolio is. How cool that we get to meet one of the actors before we leave," Ginny said.

"As many times as I've seen Romeo and Juliet," I said, "I loved this one best because it really highlighted the adolescent camaraderie between Romeo, Benvolio and Mercutio – the 'guy' antics and the search for women by young men. The Festival is really masterful at making old chestnuts new, don't you agree?"

"I'm impressed, that's for sure," Ginny said. "We never dreamt there was such world-class theatre here. They say that "All the Way" is headed to Broadway! That's so impressive. And we got to see it here!"

"It is exciting, that's for sure. And we get to go to the theatre all the time," I said.

"What I don't understand is how you get the energy to do *anything* else," Liz said. "We're all just so impressed with how you do all you do. The cooking, the supervising, the interaction with guests, problem solving, shopping. There's so much. When you left the East Coast, I don't think any of us ever realized what you were taking on."

"She's right, Donnan[2]. Here you'd lived your whole lives on the East Coast and you took off for Oregon, of all places," Betsy said. "None of us could believe it. You were *sixty*!"

---

[2]   Donnan is my "real" name, a family name I enjoy having but am rarely called by anyone but relatives anymore.

"That's true, you were," Liz said. "And I'm a landscaper and if you're doing all this gardening -- I counted 18 separate gardens -- you need more help. They may be small or just be borders, but they all need constant attention. You're going to burn out, that's what I worry about."

I immediately felt overwhelmed. *Was Liz saying the gardens were in bad shape? Was Betsy saying we were too old? Was Ginny saying we'd undertaken too much? Was everyone saying we shouldn't have left the East Coast?* I took a few deep breaths, remembering my Yoga teacher's advice. And then a slug of wine.

"Hey you guys…this isn't brain surgery, what we're doing. And we're not decrepit. It does take energy, but we find it energizing, really. But listen, you're really going to like Benvolio," I said. "And I'm sorry you won't meet my best actor friend, Catherine Coulson. When we found each other, it was like lost sisters reunited."

David and I had known this particular "Benvolio" for a long time. And the younger staff at Anne Hathaway's had identified Kevin Fugaro as "handsome and hot" even before they knew he had been on "Nurse Jackie." The fact that he was obviously a good actor was practically beside the point; they looked forward to his visits because of his good looks and how nice he was.

We knew him as the young son of our long-time guests-turned-good-friends, Steve and Jill Fugaro. The Fugaros started coming early in our tenure at Anne Hathaway's. We'd first bonded over the discovery that Jill's grandfather was the former editor of the newspaper in Western Pennsylvania where David got his first reporting job right out of college. We both knew Jimmy Murrin. Retired by the time we arrived as newlyweds, he'd been a sage and wise counsel to two rookies drowning in the fishbowl of life in a very small town. Nothing we did went unnoticed. Jimmy regularly confirmed our suspicion of same when we ran into him on the street.

Biscuit, their beloved golden retriever who accompanied them, left a lasting footprint on Anne Hathaway's. She'd become ill during their stay, so we referred them to our vet and provided safe harbor when it became clear their long-treasured pet wasn't going to make it. His compassionate end-of-life care couldn't have been more empathetic. Since dogs have always been a central feature of our lives, we understood how devastating it can be to bid farewell to one. Truly a sacred time.

For several years, Kevin joined his parents for their annual week at the Inn, when he didn't have to stay in New York for acting commitments. The staff was always disappointed if he didn't come *or* when he brought a girl-friend. Everything changed the winter when we got an excited call from Jill to announce that Kevin had been cast by the Oregon Shakespeare Festival and would shortly be moving to Ashland to take up his role of Benvolio in *Romeo and Juliet*.

"We're ecstatic," Jill said. "We can't believe it. He was the last actor hired. You're going to be seeing a lot more of us this year."

"How great," I said. "We'll get to see you two more regularly *and* Kevin can become one of our Actors at Breakfast."

Soon it was apparent that Kevin's good fortune was going to help fill any vacant rooms we might have available. No sooner had Jill written with a schedule of the trips she and Steve planned to make to Ashland during the season, than calls started coming in. Kevin's Sunday school teacher, who said he had been a natural as Joseph at age seven. Aunts and uncles and neighbors all planned to make the trek to Ashland to see their favorite Shakespearean actor. Jill's garden club, book club and college roommates put together an October trip. The list kept growing. Kevin's employment seemed to be the newest source of patrons for both the Inn and OSF. As only a proud mother would, Jill saw *Romeo and Juliet* eight times.

Kevin was an instant hit at breakfast, and not only among the staff. Guests were taken by his natural charm and charisma, eager to know as much as possible about his life on stage.

"How did you get to be Benvolio as well as an understudy for *Animal Crackers* and *Troilus and Cressida?*"

"They said they wanted someone who could be Hispanic or Middle Eastern, was sort of swarthy and could sing and dance," Kevin said. "During my try-out, they didn't say anything about needing an Irish-Italian mix like me, but what's exciting is this director's interpretation of the play. It's one we've all known since high school, but he really brings out the darkness *and* the light of very young love."

"Do the teenagers wait for you backstage?" one older guest asked.

"No, they wait for Romeo, though. He's got the teeny bopper market cornered," Kevin said.

"Ah, Kevin, you're just being modest," I said. I enjoyed playing Resident Mom, bursting with a pride I shared with his mother.

Kevin lowered his voice. "And in case you didn't notice it, Romeo and Juliet really are a couple."

"Well, is there a Juliet in *your* life," another guest asked.

Kevin cleared his voice, a frown crossed his face. I stopped for a minute to hear the answer.

"Well, um, I'm not sure I'd call her my Juliet, because, unlike the play, our families seem to like each other.." Kevin stopped for a minute and took in his breath. "But, yes, I do have a girlfriend, and she's also an actor," he said. "Now you all tell me, what's been your favorite show this season?"

Clearly, Kevin wanted a rest from the stage.

Sundays at the Inn, the menu's always the same – Rita Feinberg's Coffee Cake and The Full Oregon Breakfast (FOB). A trip to Ireland introduced us to the Full Irish Breakfast of baked beans, lightly-cooked bacon, slimy eggs, tomatoes, blood pudding and other unidentifiable items. On our way home, we decided that having a standard offering, or *tradition,* such as this, would be important. Thus was born the idea of having the FOB on a regular basis. Best of all, we could nearly always do the work for it on Saturday afternoon.

Saturday afternoon, while I was making the coffee cake, David was mixing the dozen or so ingredients for the main dish, Salmon Hash. To be honest, the signature fish of our region is not always *caught* in Oregon, but we tell guests it's probably related to one swimming in a river nearby.

At 7:30 a.m. the next day, David was squeezing all he could out of the last of the oranges. I was standing in front of our industrial-strength refrigerator, trying to add up all the guests coming for breakfast.

"There are twelve in the house, plus the cousins – that's sixteen, plus Benvolio. Seventeen. That's it," I said.

"You forgot the woman in Pomegranate," David said. "She told me she was coming."

"You're right. Then it's eighteen, including Benvolio." I opened the oven to check on the cakes and laughed, suddenly remembering the conversation from the night before.

"What's funny?" David asked.

"The cousins thought we were having something Italian for breakfast because you told them we were, 'Having Benvolio for breakfast,'" I said.

"Well, Kevin's Italian, too, so they were half right," he said.

I could tell from the noise level in the dining room that Kevin had arrived. People were introducing themselves, getting coffee, saying how much they'd enjoyed the play the night before.

Our staff members Alissa and Vieve were putting the antique milk bottles of ice water and butter plates on our trusty old table, now stretched to capacity with all five leaves. They'd added an additional table (the one where the port and sherry usually are) at one end to make it a little longer. Having unseasonably chilly weather meant we had to eat inside, and eighteen was a squeeze.

"This is what we call an 'Elbows Down Day,'" I said as I gathered guests into the dining room.

Just as people were finishing up their fruit course of poached pears, a staple of the FOB, David emerged from the kitchen to present the main dish.

"As you know, all of today's ingredients were grown in Oregon," he began. "The potatoes. The parsley. The onions and the celery. The garlic. To be honest, the salmon is actually from Alaska, but we have it on good authority that his family tree has cousins in Oregon. Until today, we've called this dish Salmon Hash. But, in honor of our star, Kevin – and Deedie's cousins – we've renamed it Salmon Benvolio! We hope you enjoy it."

On its opening morning, Salmon Benvolio got the gustatory equivalent of a standing ovation – eighteen empty plates.

As the table was being cleared and our two dishwashers loaded, I remembered I still owed Jill an email about Benvolio's "Juliet." I enclosed the recipe.

Anne Hathaway's Salmon Benvolio

Named in honor of Kevin Fugaro

- 2 medium potatoes
- 3 T butter
- 3 T oil
- 1 clove garlic
- 1 t salt
- ½ cup onion
- 1 ½ cup cooked salmon
- ½ cup celery
- 2 T bell pepper
- 4 or 5 T heavy cream
- ½ t white pepper
- ¼ cup parsley

1. Thickly slice potatoes and boil five or six minutes. Dry, cut into cubes and cook in skillet with 1 T butter and 1 T oil until golden and crispy. Transfer to bowl.

2. Dice onion, celery, garlic, peppers and cook in 1 T butter and 1 T oil until soft. Add to potatoes.

3. Stir in cream, salt and white pepper and mix. Let cool to room temperature or, if doing ahead of time, put in the fridge for the night.

4. Mix parsley and salmon into the potato mixture and cook in skillet with 1 T butter and 1 T oil until heated and slightly crispy, at least four minutes.

Feeding the Staff

I thought my physician was calling about my blood count, but it was about another patient of hers instead.

"You may have seen the news coverage about Wanda," she said, after learning that we were in fact hiring for the upcoming season. "All I can tell you is she is just about the most honest and hard working person I've ever met. Killing her husband was something she did to save her children from being killed. I've had her clean my house and can attest to her skills. The problem is, as you can imagine, there aren't many job opportunities for her just now, and I've heard the trial could be months and months away."

Pausing for a few seconds to scroll through my thoughts, my words emerged. "I did see that story. We do need someone right now. It's early in the season and the few people we have returning aren't able to come back yet." *While we had certainly "taken chances" on staff before, this was definitely a new level. What would guests think, if they found out?* "Have her call me," I said.

Bright blue as an early spring sky, Wanda's eyes made radar contact with my grey blue ones as we sat across the desk from each other a day later. Eye contact and firm handshakes rank high on my criteria when I'm hiring. Her hair pulled back so tight in a ponytail it must have hurt, her jeans pressed crisply and an ironed white shirt, Wanda presented well. No one who hadn't seen her on local television would guess she'd murdered her husband less than a month before.

Her words, as clear as her eyes, seemed to soothe her as much as they did me. "Dr. Shirley probably told you a little bit about my legal situation," she said. "I've never been in a fix like this before. I've always worked hard and had good jobs and been a good mom. And I feel as if I did the only thing I could have done in the situation, even though I know it's wrong to take anyone's life away from them," she said. Then, in a rush, she said, "I don't know if you know this or not, but my husband had already murdered our dogs. My children and me were next in line and we all knew it."

I thought I saw some water filling those spellbinding eyes. I definitely felt my own beginning to tear, as they always do when I'm confronted with the human toll domestic violence extracts. Like an item on a discarded grocery list at the bottom of your pocketbook, the term *domestic violence* ends up on the floor of our minds unless we see its reality up close. This was not my first encounter with it, but as grisly as they get.

"Dr. Shirley says you're good people and I can promise you right now I'll do a good job here. I'm totally honest. I've done housekeeping before. 'Even been the Head Housekeeper at that La Quinta out on the I-5, but of course they had to let me go when I was arrested. It's a long drive for me to get here, but it would be a good job and that's what I need right now."

We had had an unexpected surge of early theatregoers this particular year and had little help. I was already exhausted from doing more housekeeping than I had for a number of years. I still knew how to clean a toilet, but I was resenting it more with each passing day. We needed help!

And here came Wanda before we even had to advertise. I told David about Shirley's call.

"Don't forget our agreement from last season," he said. "I'm sure Wanda's really good, but didn't we say we were out of the social work business? She's going to need a lot of help besides an income," he said.

"I know, I know. But Shirley is convinced she won't be a burden. She says she wouldn't have asked otherwise. And now that I've met her, I have no hesitation at all. Promise."

The agreement to which David referred was reached at the end of the prior season: We needed to concentrate on being innkeepers and employ-ers, **not** social workers. The foregoing season featured such a diversity of *issues* each staff member was dealing with rather than actual diversity (which is hard to come by in small-town Oregon) that we were constantly juggling the *personal* needs of nearly every staff member. Maybe because we'd always had bunches of kids floating in and out of our house as our chil-dren grew up, to whom we'd become advisors, but we'd unwittingly fallen into the same pattern with some staff members that season. Problems with your parents? *Here's my advice.* Don't you think you ought to see a doctor about your hair loss? *Here, I can give you the name of one.* Transgender? I don't know much about it. *But there must be a counseling center at the University.* Problems getting along with the other staff? *You might consider sharing fewer personal opinions about the quality of their work. And also, deodorant is a good thing to use when it's so hot. Here, we have some in the I Forgot Box -- you can have it for your own.* My personal favorite peren-nial excuse from one housekeeper was "abdominal migraines." When they came on her, it made sweeping and vacuuming and standing difficult. I advised her to do her job or quit, suddenly hardnosed.

There was the issue of how Wanda would interact with guests and other staff. Her amazing authenticity overcame my fears after a few moments of thought.

"Wanda, it seems like you would be a good fit here," I said. "No matter what your legal situation is. You certainly know what it takes to keep things clean and tidy and the guests happy. You have experience. And you've been recommended by someone we highly respect. Any chance you could you start tomorrow?"

"Sure thing, Miss Deedie. I promise not to disappoint you *or* Dr. Shirley. What time?" Wanda could have been doing a scene from a training film. Her face intent, her person very present and the biggest smile I'd seen since I met her.

Watching Wanda tackle one task after another, with ease, replaced our early-season angst with delight. Along the way, she kept discovering other things that needed to be done, "if you don't mind, Miss Deedie." For the first time, cobwebs and dust in hard-to-reach corners disappeared before we ever saw them. We would never have known the Dollar Store is where to buy heavy starch (a mainstay for table linens) were it not for Wanda. She even wanted to know if I would *mind* if she did some weeding! *What karmic favor had we performed to deserve Wonderful Wanda, as we referred to her?*

Possessed of endless good cheer, not to mention equanimity about her dreadful situation, she regularly shared updates on her children and also on the progress of "her case" with us. Local and national Women's Rights and Domestic Abuse advocacy groups angled to be her lead defense, to her surprise.

Wanda was signing out one afternoon around two. I was eating my salad at the desk and trying to get out confirmation letters.

"You have a minute to hear the latest, Miss Deedie?"

"Sure. Sit down," I said.

This is going to be a real long process. No telling when the trial will be or how long it'll take. It makes me dizzy. I just want it all behind me."

"I sure can understand that, Wanda, but please remember what an incredibly important service you're doing for so, so many other women out there. As I already told you, David's sister was killed by her husband before *she* ever had a chance to speak out."

"I know, Miss Deedie, I know. But I have to think of my kids, too."

We inherited our third child, five-year-old Sara, as the result of a mur-der-suicide. The pain and grief we all suffered at Susan Runkel's death was exacerbated in a major way -- to this moment -- by the fact that we knew it was a possibility and didn't act to prevent it. Like us, Susan knew it was a possibility and was also helpless.

So Wanda was not our first experience with domestic abuse. What impressed us was her courage in taking action in defense of herself and her children.

As the season ramped up and we brought more staff on board, Wanda continued as our awesome anchor. Being a major tourist destination and also a college town, there is generally a good supply of housekeepers from which to choose in Ashland. That said, jobs at Anne Hathaway's are com-petitive because we start people at more than minimum wage. We don't want anyone who works for us to think they are saddled with a "just a minimum wage" job.

The interviewing process for high school and University students is not unlike Congressional hearings for Supreme Court candidates. "What's been the most difficult case you've ever had to deal with?" "Do you real-ize this is an extremely detail-oriented job?" "Are you a quick learner?" For Wanda, I'd left out the questions about why she left her last job or whether she had a criminal record. "How do you get along with your fel-low workers?" Running through the back of my head was "How will they do with Wanda?"

It was a relief to face the season with so few "issues" at the outset. We declared our career as social worker/employers officially over, unless you counted Wanda, which we didn't.

Not only that, but our new team all wanted to know what they should wear to work, a welcome concern after a season or two of high goth and lime green high heels, among other things. We already had Anne Hathaway's aprons, but maybe we should try something different.

"What do you think about having a dress code?" I asked David one night.

"Don't you think that's getting a little too formal? It's not as if we're TSA or Federal Express," he said.

"Here's what I think -- if the staff wants them, let's get them! We're here to make their job easier and make them proud of working here. I propose we get polo shirts with the Anne Hathaway's logo on them."

David thought for a while. "How's that going to make it easier to get rid of the bellies and bottoms we sometimes get to see on the hotter days?"

"Easy," I said. "No bottoms or bellies *ever* showing, and here are your own beautiful shirts."

I ordered them online that night in all different colors. When they arrived the following week, people were more delighted than I'd thought possible when I handed them out, along with the bellies and bottoms rule. "No more having to worry about getting bleach on your best shirt," I said. I couldn't help noticing what color each person chose. Wanda a cherry red one, Robin, yellow. Theo took white. Claire wanted grey, Colleen navy, Ellen, blue, Alissa, purple. It somehow made sense -- Wanda always cheerful, Robin always sunny, Theo sterile and white.

Celebrating the middle of the season by taking everyone out to lunch has become a tradition for us. Early in our innkeeping careers, we realized that the housekeeping staff is literally the most important element to our achieving success. Forget about how tasty the food is or how beautiful the gardens were. No matter how charming we are as hosts or pleasing the interior decorating, *if there is hair in the bathtub (or, horrors, elsewhere), or dust bunnies under the bed, the guests will not return.* So, we tell all our housekeepers at the outset, they have the most important job at Anne Hathaway's. We both came to our innkeeping career with pretty good backgrounds in recruiting, management, hiring and firing when necessary and have always shared the belief that our job is to serve our staff so they can do their job well. Taking everyone out to lunch is an exercise in this philosophy. It also helps build "the team," another one of our goals.

"You don't have to love each other, but we do insist you treat each other with respect," I say to each person as we bring them on board. "That means no gossiping or hypercritical remarks."

We embarked on the walk to this particular year's edition of the staff lunch on a beastly hot July afternoon. All the rooms had (I'd been assured) been cleaned, bathrooms sanitized, porches swept, flowers watered and kitchen left sparkling. We all met in front of the Inn and began the one-block journey to Pasta Piatti, a local bistro. For most, this was a first, for a few others, their third or fourth year they'd been a member of a Team Hathaway trip to the restaurant. I hurried ahead to put place cards out at each place, along with the small gift books I'd selected and wrapped for each person, keyed to something I was pretty sure they'd be interested in. Colleen got a handbook about local Native Americans, some of whose blood ran in her veins, she regularly averred; Alissa got a book about home brewing so she and her husband could make gluten-free beer; Theo got an "Anatomy for Dummies" in recognition of his taking Basic Anatomy for the fourth – and we hoped final – time. (Theo's chief goal in life was to become a wrestling coach. The basic anatomy course was a prerequisite to getting the necessary degree in physical education at the local university.) Sometimes when I encountered him, I'd point to one of my less-well-known muscles and ask him to name it. Robin got a book of running trails in the region. The notebook of English Stratfordshire bull terriers was instantly cherished by Claire, who had two of the species. Wanda got a book of inspiring quotes from women. Shopping for the perfect and strategic gift was something I loved doing each year. And everyone got a different kind of moustache to wear. I knew from experience they were definitely excellent party starters for a group that had team aspirations.

It was quite a colorful procession, our staff parade. To my dismay, Wanda was missing. One of her children had become ill and she had to rush home to take her to the doctor. Colleen, the employee with longevity in age and employment at Anne Hathaway's, acted as chief shepherd as our team made its way down tree-lined East Main Street.

Having finished his toilet cleaning duties before everyone else, Theo was already there and greeted me at the door of the restaurant.

"Hey, Theo. I was worried you were going to be intimidated by dining out with all these women," I said.

"Oh, I can do it," he said, showing me where the large table that had been set aside for us was. "All it takes is a little muscle."

"*Which* muscle?" I said, laughing.

"Theo, you did a fabulous job on those bathrooms today," Colleen said as she walked in.

"He's just plain awesome when it comes to bathrooms," Robin said. Theo demurred, putting one hand out and waving it downward. Enough about the bathrooms. We discovered early on that while Theo was a very willing worker, he excelled most at bathroom cleaning, so that's what he became the Chief Specialist in. We never like to have people doing things they either don't like to do or aren't very good at. With bed making clearly not one of his long suits and sterilized bathrooms his specialty, it made sense to crown him bathroom king. Sue declared she constitutionally couldn't be pleasant early in the mornings, so she never ever got to share her morning scowl with breakfast guests.

The day before the big luncheon, Colleen, whom we'd asked to act as an assistant manager, had reported that people wanted to know if they had to wear their "uniforms" to the party.

"I guess not," I said. "We want people to have fun and maybe they wouldn't think they could have fun if they have to wear their 'work' clothes. Tell them they can wear whatever they want to. Party clothes, if they want to."

Most of them wore their official polo shirts.

Finally, everyone was seated and studying their menus, their moustaches making them appear all the more serious. I went around the table doing stealth iPhone snaps of the hilarious scene, as experience told me the sticky moustaches would soon begin to itch and be removed. David and I assured everyone at our opposite ends of the table they could order anything they wanted from the menu. The waiters came to take orders and suddenly everyone was silent. Were they so used to *providing* service they didn't know how to *be* served?

"C'mon, everyone. Order up whatever you want," I waved my menu. "There're so many good things. The Italian polpette is my favorite."

The surprisingly laborious ordering process finally completed, I tapped my water glass with my knife to get everyone's attention. "I want to hear from each of you what your favorite moment's been so far this season, okay?" I said. "We'll go around the table. And David, you and I get to tell also. Why don't you start, Colleen? You've worked here the longest."

"She's right. I was actually on the front porch the day Deedie and David pulled in the driveway in their light green Passat wagon, all the way from Washington, DC. You wouldn't believe what a long way they've come since then," she said animatedly, then paused. "I'm really torn about my most favorite moment, so I think I'll tell two."

I waved my Boss Finger at her and said, "Only One, Only One."

She continued, undaunted. The first was the day Deedie checked someone into a room and found a couple already in there taking a nap. (*Well, that's what she said they were doing.*) [Laughter] Boy, were they surprised. And Deedie was so shocked. It was *hysterical*. Fortunately, we had another room available for the check-ins so we could leave the love birds to themselves."

I shuddered. And then smiled at the memory that my first instinct had been to let Cole Porter do the talking -- "Birds do it, even very educated fleas do it." But my nerve abandoned me and I reached an advanced state of mortification instead. *Mortifying, Colleen, this was definitely not hysterical.* But those very same loving guests were back this year, I thought, so they must not have cared too much that I invaded their (under the covers, fortunately) intimacy

Colleen continued way too enthusiastically. "Then, there was the day when there was nothing made yet for teatime at 4 and it was already 3:15. Suddenly, Deedie says, 'Fruit pizza!' as if I knew what she was talking about. Next thing I knew, I'd been sent out the back door to Safeway and within *half an hour* she'd created an extraordinary, incredibly tasty big pizza using five different fruits covering a cookie crust. I'm telling you it was a Martha Stewart deal in *living color.* Here's how she did it -- you won't believe it."

By this time, I could see that people an advanced state of boredom brought on by Colleen's filibuster showed signs of setting in. *All my fault for calling on her first.* I tried to hasten the conclusion by looking at her hard and winding my finger a little, referee style. She appeared undeterred.

"I don't think we need to give them the whole recipe, Colleen. What made it so good for you?" David broke in.

"Oh, that's easy. Because it was so delicious and the guests were so happy. It literally disappeared. I just want to say I think Deedie's amazing because she can take all kinds of different ingredients -- food or human beings -- that you can't imagine putting together and make it come out good," she said, putting her hands down hard in front of her.

Obedient, albeit light, applause.

Alissa's favorite moment came when she got the tee shirts and didn't have to worry about what to wear to work. Robin said it was the day one of the guests picked her up when her bike had a flat tire and she was walking to work. "They even put my bike in the back of their car!" Theo said his favorite moment was when he'd been crowned Bathroom King and therefore didn't have to make any more beds. "And also, I've gotten some coaching on anatomy from the owners," he said with a smile.

Ellen's favorite story was her hiring. "I stopped Deedie on the street one day and told her they were cutting back my hours at the theatre and I was a pretty good baker."

"Come with me," she said, turning me around. "Ten minutes later, I was making muffins in the big kitchen at the Inn."

"And we had the relief cook we knew we needed," I said.

Ellen got a muffin cookbook.

"Hey, where's Wanda?" Robin broke in. Everyone started looking around, saying, "Yeah, where's Wanda?"

Colleen waited for the buzz to die down and then told about the doctor appointment. "She's so cool, isn't she?" she said.

There was instant general, and what seemed totally genuine, agreement, then applause.

"I saved her a moustache," Claire said.

"What did she get for a present?" Alissa asked. I thought for a moment and then decided to reveal the title of Wanda's present.

"Hers is a book of quotes by women. Its title is "Women Take a Stand," I said, looking from face to face. Everyone clapped. I hadn't been sure until that moment if everyone knew about Wanda's "situation," but apparently they did, as everyone started talking animatedly. About how much they loved Wanda. And what they'd heard about her on the radio, the television and on the street.

"Deedie, isn't there anything the rest of us can do for Wanda? We all want to," Alissa said. "We've all been talking about her courage and her situation and how hard she works and we want to do something to help her or her kids."

'I'll talk to her tomorrow, but my guess is she's going to be reluctant," I said. "All this attention is hard for her. I think she's embarrassed and maybe a little shy."

While I wasn't surprised that there was so much support for her from the staff, I was moved by the depth of what people said. Obviously, most of their information had come from the media.

"They say she could end up in jail for a long time," Robin said, tears welling in her eyes.

"I'm a Christian like Wanda is," Ellen said, taking off her big black-rimmed glasses and rubbing her eyes, "but as far as I'm concerned, what she did was in self-defense, and that's just it."

"That dude she killed, he deserved it, doesn't matter if you're a Christian or not," Theo said. "I haven't talked to her about it, but that's what I believe."

When Wanda came to work the next day, she asked for some private time to share some news. I worried there might be something seriously the matter with her daughter, the last thing in the world she needed. She came into the office, closed the door gently and sat down across from me, eyes closed, almost as if in prayer. Raising her eyes until they caught mine and locked in, she said, "I'm going to jail. I have to quit. I can't finish the season, even though I know I promised you I would if I could. I'm really, really sorry to disappoint you, Miss Deedie."

"But Wanda," I said. "There hasn't even been a trial yet. You can't automatically assume you're headed to jail. You have so much support."

"You're right, I can't. But it's come to me over these last months just how hard a trial would be on me and my kids. We've all started to move beyond this nightmare. And heal. We have *so* much healing to do, Miss Deedie." She tossed her head back, spraying her ponytail into the air momentarily. "Going through a trial would bring it all back. We'd be in the thick of it all over again, day after day. Besides, I'm a religious woman and I did do something very wrong. You know as well as I do that one of the Ten Commandments is, 'Thou shalt not kill.' I should have to pay *something* for it. Don't you see?" I pushed my chair in and reached out to hold one of her hands, gripping it tightly. Tears flowed.

"The kids understand that -- they're Christians too. And their grandmother, their father's mother, is going to take care of them. I just know it's the right thing to do and I hope you and David can understand. You've been really good to me," she finished and got up to come around the desk toward me.

I began to cry harder than I had been as we hugged each other. I felt Wanda's bony shoulder bones shimmy with a sob.

"It'll be okay, Miss Deedie. I just know it. This is all God's will. And I'll write to you. I promise. I like to write letters."

When the rest of the staff learned Wanda would be leaving, they wanted to have a party for her. Wanda didn't want one. Instead, she collected everyone's address in an address book we gave her in a mini-farewell ceremony. Once everyone had written down their address, we gathered for a porch picture.

"I promise to write each of you," she said. "And please write back. I'm thinking I'm going to get pretty lonely up there. And please send this picture so I can show the others."

At the end of the season, three months into Wanda's incarceration, David and I had one of our "business meetings," a practice we'd put in place after our marriage counseling as a way to keep our personal and professional issues separate.

"What do we want to do better next year?" David asked. "How do you feel about how it all worked out with the staff? You're the one who puts the most energy into that."

"I think it's worth all the energy, because everything turns out okay in the end. It's sort of like all the slicing you have to do for a good soup – or a fruit pizza – when you put it all together and cook it just right, it tastes good and looks even better," I said. "I'm feeling pretty darn good about the staff. They *are* the most important part of our operation and that guest was right when she said it pays to help them some, *and* to pay them well to help."

"Absolutely right. I agree," he said. "By the way, did you see we got a letter from Wanda today? That's two this week. Alissa also got one, and so did Claire."

"Today's letter reports she's learning Spanish from her non-English-speaking cellmate in return for giving her Bible lessons. She says they can communicate because they're sisters in Christ," David said.

"You know," I said, "I've always thought the saying, 'Everything happens for a reason' was just about the most trite thing anyone could say. Between Wanda's deep faith in God being the Master of her universe and there being a reason for every event, I can actually feel my own faith being restored through her," I said.

We hugged for a long time. Our years of being social workers and parents to our employees may have ended. But now we had Wanda, who had many lessons to teach us. Even after more than 50 years of marriage.

Wanda served 11 months of a three-year sentence, three months in a pre-release program and is now back with her family.

Fruit Pizza

From dear friend Geraldine Male

Ingredients

- 2 rolls of Pillsbury sugar cookie dough (the ONLY ready-made ingredient in any of our recipes.)
- 1/12 packages of cream cheese
- 1/3 cup sugar
- Dollop of plain yogurt or sour cream
- Zest of two lemons
- 2 T. lemon juice
- Strawberries, blueberries, blackberries, bananas, peaches, grapes…whatever fresh fruit you can lay your hands on. Do NOT use frozen.

Directions -- Preheat oven to 350.

1. Cut rolls of cookie dough into approximately ¼" slices. Arrange about ¼" apart on large pizza pan that has been sprayed liberally with your spray of choice. If it's one of those with holes in it, cover with parchment so dough doesn't seep through those holes. Bake until light brown and lovely. Cool as completely as you can given time constraints.

2. Beat the cream cheese, sugar, lemon juice, zest and juice until smooth and creamy.

3. Arrange all that fruit as artfully, tastefully and Stewartfully (you know who I'm talking about) as you possibly can. This step often offers a photo opportunity for Facebook.

4. If you like glazes, melt some of your favorite jam and droozle it over the pie (some find *tart* a more appropriate name for this confection).

N.B. At this point, we do not offer a gluten-free alternative to this item. Nor do I think we ever will. It just wouldn't taste good.

Anne Hathaway's
Breakfast Club Band

Stand beside her, and guide her. The Mormon Tabernacle Choir burst forth through speakers placed in the kitchen windows with "God Bless America." Judy, her long red hair blowing in the early morning breeze, led twenty people down the driveway, all pounding pans with wooden spoons, or clanging pot lids and singing along. I was last in line, laughing too hard to sing one of my favorite songs.

With no drum major, when our raucous revelers got to the street, they turned around and marched back up the driveway. As the Anne Hathaway's Breakfast Club Band reached the end of its route and began -- somewhat reluctantly -- to disassemble, I noticed two sleepy-looking figures emerging from the house next door, blinking in the sunlight. There they were, Jon and Chris, our neighbors and favorite college students.

News of a party in their yard the night before had greeted me the moment I arrived for work that morning from our condo down the street Apparently, no one in the house had been spared the clamor emanating from next door. What had started as soft guitar music and loudish voices burgeoned into a boisterous crowd. One guest after another dropped by the kitchen to share with me their own experience of the unexpected hullabaloo, and their own sleepless night.

"In our room, it was as if the party were right here in the Inn," Shirley said, interrupting Judy, who was in the middle of telling everyone that her husband was going to be hell to deal with all day because he could not tolerate being awakened in the middle of the night.

"I'm really sorry to hear all these reports," I said, putting the fresh scones down on the counter in the dining room. People clustered around the table getting coffee, talking about their personal experiences with the party gang. "I wish someone had called us and we would have gone over. We know these kids and they do have different hours than we do, but we've never had a problem like this before," I said.

"Don't worry about it, Deedie," Shirley said. "These things happen."

"I sure hope they don't happen again or my husband won't let us come back to Ashland," Judy said.

I returned to the kitchen an unhappy innkeeper. The more I thought about it, the more aggravated I got. *This was almost as bad as bedbugs (a noun I'd vowed never to say out loud) because it was something I couldn't control*! I felt like we'd entered a danger zone.

As I collected the ingredients for oatmeal soufflés, I heard the conversation start again in the dining room. Someone was telling about the chickens next door to where they lived and all the noise *they* made.

I told David we had a situation and we needed a strategy to deal with it. "We can't have those kids keeping the guests up all night," I said. "You should hear them talking out there."

"Don't worry, Deedie. It'll blow over," David said. As he spoke, he laid strips of bacon on the large griddle. Bacon is always a hit in spite of its bad reputation. We can never cook enough.

"Oh, I'm sure it will blow over at some point, but we really have to speak to those boys," I said. "And I think it should be you who does it. Male-to-male."

The two young men next door were our friends. We'd watched Jon and Chris progress through three years of college as art majors. We'd housed their parents when they came to visit, and commiserated with them as parents can do. The boys' creativity was not at all confined to their art. Always on the alert for a scheme to fund their next semester or project, they proved more inventive than Steve Jobs, who they worshiped. For a while, it was silk-screened tee shirts they made in the backyard and sold on Craig's List. When Chris needed discarded computer parts for a big installation he was building, a sign went up promising free disposal of same. An electronic trash pile grew into an unsightly mess overnight, lasting two weeks. One lazy Sunday afternoon, they sponsored a talent show in the backyard, for which their friends paid a cover charge for unlimited beer and fragrant dope. Our chocolate lab, Hattie, made her debut in one of the acts, showing off her ball catching prowess wearing a pink tutu. Neither the boys nor Hattie had let us know in advance that she'd been auditioned. Fortunately, that event ended by nine o'clock.

Jon's most ambitious money-making scheme had been presented to us as an investment opportunity -- and a menu item. Would we be interested in buying some of the oyster mushrooms they'd be bringing back from a hunting and prospecting trip to Arizona? Many of the toniest restaurants in Ashland had already bought in, he said. Sauteed oyster mushroom crepes would work, he suggested. Our food budget couldn't afford such high-end ingredients, but we congratulated them on their indefatigable ingenuity. And after they returned, we took guests to view the ruins of the $2,000 cache they'd carefully spread out on a huge blue tarp with another tarp over them. Given all the moisture in the air and in the mushrooms themselves, these fabulous fungi rotted in no time at all. We felt so bad for them that we purchased one of Jon's six-foot ceramic constructions to help with the resulting shortfall.

Our impromptu driveway band found its calling during breakfast in the garden, the morning after the party. Eighteen weary guests had assembled for breakfast, scattered among three tables. This was my favorite point every morning, seeing people sit down and comment on how perfectly beautiful everything looked.

"Do you suppose they pick the flowers every day to match the table-cloths?" a new guest asked.

"I saw one of the girls out here this morning looking for flowers to cut," Ardis, who had been coming for four years, assured her. "See how each place has its own little vase with its own little arrangement?"

When I returned with juice, conversation was still about The Party.

"Not only was I a teacher, but I raised four boys," Judy said, taking credit for having put an end to things last night. "I lay there in bed for just so long and then I said to myself, 'This is not going to end unless I do something, and our room's the closest to the scene of action.'"

"So what did you do?" I asked.

"I opened our window and yelled, 'HEY!' at the top of my lungs. Nothing happened. My husband said I should give up. But I tried again. 'HEY!' That one got heard. Things got a little quieter, but not quiet enough as far as I was concerned."

I hurried away. The boys had really done us a disservice. Surely they knew better, I thought. How could they *not* have imagined they'd wake our guests? *Thoughtless, self-centered, over-privileged kids, just like mine were in the day.*

I turned on the oven light to see how all those soufflés were doing. A tinge of brown crept across the tops of each one nicely. David was unloading the griddle and preparing another batch of bacon.

"David, you'll be interested to know that Judy is the heroine of the day. She says she stopped the party singlehandedly."

"What did she do? Turn the hose on them?" he asked.

"No, but what a great idea," I said. "I wish I'd thought of that. I'm so mad at them right now I feel like turning the hose on them!"

The timer went off for the soufflés. They all appeared beautifully browned, tall and substantial, worthy of a photograph in *Gourmet* magazine.

With a nice purple scabiosa and a fresh cantaloupe slice from the garden on each plate, we started carrying the plates out, walking slowly lest our puffy cargo fall.

Oooh's and Ah's came from every table. "Deedie, I don't know where you get the nerve to make this many soufflés at once," Francie Gass said. "I would be so afraid."

"You get used to it after a while," I said, putting each plate down gently. In no time, the soufflés were a thing of the past. Returning to the kitchen for more coffee, I met David carrying an armload of pots and a bunch of wooden spoons. "What in heaven's name are these?" I asked.

" We have to pay these boys back. They're sleeping and our poor guests are sleep-deprived and mad. It'll be good therapy for everyone, don't you think? It's called 'retribution'!"

I smiled. "What a GREAT idea. Perfect!"

"You go ahead and make the announcement," he said, putting down his pans and spoons. After I was sure the guests were completely done eating, I banged on the metal table with one of the wooden spoons.

"Listen up, everyone. Listen up! David has thought of a great act of retribution and redemption and we're all going to participate. While you're all out here talking about the sleep you missed last night, the party boys are over there sound asleep. We figure we can bring a little justice to this neighborhood and give them a dose of their own medicine," I announced, holding up a pot and a wooden spoon. "C'mon. Join Anne Hathaway's Breakfast Club Band!" I started banging my pot a little.

In no time at all, every pan was taken. Our staff person Camelia went inside and returned with lids to make into cymbals and handed them out to the rest of our musicians.

"So what's the occasion?" Jon asked laconically when I arrived in their yard. He was trying to clean his glasses on his tee shirt, which was still covered with red clay dirt from the mushroom fiasco.

"David thought it would be a good way to remind you guys not to let your parties keep our guests awake at night," I said. "I know we're friends, but you've got to remember we're running a business here."

Jon shook his head 'yes.' "I'm sorry, Deedie, David," he said, looking toward Chris, whose head was down.

"Honestly, we felt pretty good about cleaning up all the beer bottles because we know you don't like your guests to have to see *them*," Chris said.

"Yup, I noticed that," I said. "Thanks."

"Guys, the problem really was the noise. See all these people here? They're as tired as you are, and they're on vacation," David said, patting my shoulder.

By now, the guests had gone back to their rooms. A few had sat back down and were having another cup of coffee. I had the sense they wanted to witness our neighborhood drama as it played out.

"See, what happened was, our friends arrived in the middle of the night and I guess it was sort of an impromptu party," Jon said.

"We really didn't plan it and we're sorry," Chris added.

"Thanks for the apology and also for cleaning up the bottles. But you know, any more loud parties and we could lose business, big time," I said.

"I got it, Deedie. We're sorry," Jon said again, turning to go back inside. "I hope this doesn't mean we aren't going to get leftovers anymore."

"We're not going to cut you off *this* time," David said.

A few days later, I answered the door. It was a young woman in very short shorts and a tank top. Jon stood by her side.

"Hi, Deedie," Jon said. "Tricia's our neighbor on the other side and she wants to talk to you."

"C'mon in," I said.

Tricia began talking immediately. "We're having a party tonight and Chris and Jon told us it could be a problem with your guests, so maybe, we were thinking, we could give you and your guests our phone numbers and if there's *any problem at all with noise,* maybe someone could call us and we'll be sure to quiet things down immediately." She took a deep breath, pushed her thick blonde hair away from her face and looked up at me. She handed me a three by five card with four telephone numbers carefully printed on it.

"That's really thoughtful of you. Just be sure you keep the volume down," I said. "We'll let people know and you have a good party, okay?"

"They don't want to risk a visit from your band," Jon whispered under his breath to me.

"We will, we will have a good, quiet party," Tricia said. As she turned to go down the porch steps, I heard an audible sigh.

Jon threw his hand over her shoulder like he just had on mine and said, "See, I told you she was really nice."

The following Spring, two large ivory envelopes arrived addressed to David and me. I opened one while David opened the other, curious as to what they contained.

"Hey, this is great!" David exclaimed, extracting his invitation to commencement exercises at Southern Oregon University before I did. Both Jon and Chris had invited us to the ceremony where their degrees would be conferred.

Jon had told us during the winter that if he did graduate, it would be a miracle.

And Chris had said he wasn't sure he was going to stick around for the actual ceremony.

"This is nearly as good as having our own kids graduate," I said. "We have to go!"

"Maybe we should offer to bring our instruments," David said with his big smile and a twinkle in both his very blue eyes.

Oatmeal Soufflés

- Makes 3
- *1 C milk*
- *2 T butter*
- ¾ C regular oatmeal
- ½ t salt
- ½ t freshly-grated nutmeg
- ½ t cinnamon
- ½ C light brown sugar
- *1/3 C cream cheese*
- *4 eggs*

Preheat oven 350F; Butter three 1-cup soufflé dishes.

1. In a large saucepan or Dutch oven, bring the milk and butter to a gentle simmer.
2. Add the salt and oatmeal and cook for five minutes.
3. Off the heat stir in the spices, brown sugar, and cream cheese.
4. Separate the eggs and add the yolks to the oatmeal mixture, stirring well
5. Beat the egg whites stiff. Add 1/3 of the egg whites to the oatmeal and beat in to lighten the mixture.
6. Gently fold in the remaining egg whites. Spoon the mixture into the three soufflé dishes.
7. Put the soufflé dishes on a baking sheet and carefully transfer to the oven. Bake for 20-25 minutes.

Note: Steps 1-5 may be done 30-60 minutes ahead. Do not beat egg whites until just before folding and baking.

Salsa Alegria

Tran. - Happiness, joy, gladness; contentment, satisfaction

S omehow I'd already forgotten what we'd learned in marriage counseling the morning after our last session. David and I were alone in the kitchen.

"I can't believe you did it again," I said.

"What did I do now?" David asked.

"You told me I used the wrong griddle to cook the sausages on and now they wouldn't have the grill marks like they should. I hate it when you correct me in front of the staff and you know it and besides, who said you were the expert on cooking sausages the *right* way? And also, what the hell difference does it make if they have grill marks or not? And by the way, Happy Birthday." I walked up behind him and patted his back, hopeful that it might help dissolve our difference of the moment. But nervous.

"Thanks. Well, if you'd just listen to what I say, everything would be all right. You *never* listen to me!" he came right back. *So much for my peacemaking effort.*

Feeling wounded as I always felt when David accused me of anything, I left to take the coffee and cream to the dining room. Some of our favorite guests were here. A family of five Cuban siblings and their spouses.

"Good morning, Deedie," Gus said. "What incredibly delectable dish are we having today?" he asked, watching me write out the menu on the small blackboard that sits over the bar.

Hmm, I thought. I hope Gus didn't hear our sausage spat.

"Well, it has a slightly Latin flavor to it....Salsa Alegria, or at least that's what we've decided to call it in honor of your family," I said. "I forget what they called it in the recipe, but we decided this was a better description."

"Well I'd say everything around here is *alegria*. We were just talking last night at dinner about how completely unflappable you and David are, and how well you get along. It's really amazing."

"Thanks, Gus. We do have our moments, though."

Tears came to my eyes as I turned to go back to work on the scones, in silence. David was busy squeezing oranges for juice. I couldn't help noticing he'd switched the sausages to the *right* griddle. While I was talking to Gus, he apparently had also mixed up the Salsa Alegria, which was waiting to go in the oven as soon as the scones came out.

Then it came to me that going silent was something David hated about my response to conflict -- and I'd pledged during one of our counseling sessions to stop using silence as a weapon.

"Hey, I thought I was doing the Salsa Alegria this morning. It looks like you did."

"I was just trying to be helpful. I knew you were pissed about the sausages so I decided to help out and make it. I was trying to *help*. Why is it that no matter what I do, you're mad?" David said.

"That's just not true, and you know it," I said. "I thought we'd agreed to abide by whatever agreements we had and this morning we agreed I was going to make the Salsa Alegria, even though you're usually the one who makes it. I bet you secretly don't think I do as good a job as you do! Just like the sausages."

"Deedie! Stop it. We've got to stop this bickering and get to work." David pulled the lever down on the orange squeezer hard.

Our good friend, Catherine E. Coulson, the leading lady in Robert Shenkkan's *By the Waters of Babylon,* which brought the Cubans to us in the first place, was coming for breakfast. She'd told me on the phone she was eager to hear directly from them their reaction to the play, in which she falls in love with her Cuban gardener. Her husband in the play, a university professor, has just died and friends have suggested she take up gardening to deal with her grief. The gardener turns out to have been a university professor in Cuba and eventually teaches her much more than gardening.

"So how does the gardener's story relate to your own stories?" Catherine asked those at her table, but in a stage voice that easily reached the other two tables.

"It definitely has the ring of truth to it," Gus answered. "Our parents were both from educated families and came here with nothing but the seven of us."

Cristina chimed in. "That's for sure. And our papa had to go from being a business owner to working in a vacuum cleaner factory when he first got here."

"Well, what did the play do for you?" Catherine asked. "Could you see parallels and changes taking place as the play went on?"

Listening in to my good friend speaking to the guests, I was afraid they'd be intimidated by what sounded to me like an interrogation. What I knew about Catherine was, though, that she loved a chance to interact with her audience and to have actual Cubans was a definite bonus. I looked around and found everyone spellbound by her. Whether it was her innate abilities as an actor or what, I learned later that every last one of the guests felt like she was speaking directly to them. I could relate.

Gus's wife Judy was the first to jump in. Since she'd been a literature major, she was always granted special authority by the others.

"Isn't the story of unexpected love a universal one, an eternal one? The gardener didn't have to be a Cuban; he could have been anyone, any background or nationality or race or a twenty-three year old – love is unexpected some times and causes magical things to happen. That's what I think," she said picking up her fork to take another bite of Salsa Alegria.

Before anyone else could get a word in about the play, the conversation shifted away from Cuba to plans for the day. I checked to be sure David wasn't in hearing range and said I hoped everyone would be back by 4:30 for David's surprise 64th birthday party. "See if you can round everyone up to come, will you please?" It took work to sound positive when I was seething just beneath the surface, not feeling inclined toward knocking myself out for my sausage despot of a husband.

"Sure will. That sounds like a great idea. Are we all going to sing 'When I'm Sixty-four'?"

"We are indeed," I said, stepping back toward the kitchen.

I had started to clear the tables with Alissa and Camelia. There wasn't a trace of the Salsa Alegria left.

Maybe my surprise birthday gesture would tear down the fence that built up between David's end of the kitchen and mine. I'd asked my choir director friend, Don Marston, to come with his keyboard so we could serenade David with "When I'm Sixty-four." Suddenly, the number 64 seemed so ancient. I love the song. But I don't think I ever imagined singing it when I *was* 64. *My dad was dead before he got to 64.* As I filled first one dishwasher and then the other, I began to wonder if other innkeepers had the same issues we did. Or had gotten counseling. *And* presented the same flawless façade in public. We'd had marriage counseling but I still let David get to me when I shouldn't. And I certainly knew I got to him. Regularly.

Getting to the marriage counseling stage took nerve. I had convinced myself that David would never hear of it. But at the end of our first four years, the 'flawless façade' had frayed and become harder and harder to maintain. Our end-of-season destination was the house of our good friends Michael and Stephen, who planned to be away. We were both looking forward to the chance to be away from phones, scones and guests. The hot tub, beautiful surroundings plus no responsibilities, a shining sun and solitude beckoned to us.

I fantasized that deep into a hike in the desert, I'd start the conversation and see where it went. I've always been the one who went to therapists. While David certainly believes that while there's benefit to be had, counseling is decidedly not one of his default positions. But I thought that being by ourselves for a week would give us the space to process and define the issues that had become an elephant that followed us around in our new undertaking.

To our surprise, Michael and Stephen had decided not to be away, leaving the week more a visit with old friends than a therapeutic recovery of any kind. They asked what it was like for us to be working together 24/7 and David responded, "We're having a great time. Innkeeping is a really good fit for us." He was right about the vocational fit, but maybe not matrimonially.

While we had a fun week exploring the desert, hiking and having meals we didn't have to fix, nary a scone to make, we had little time to ourselves and even less time to face the music of the past season.

On our way home, we'd been on the road for 709 miles, during which time we listened to *Great Expectations* and did precious little talking. The book ended, though, and now we had only ourselves. As we came around the bend to the majesty of Mt. Shasta, famous for its special energy fields, I finally got up my nerve. Only half listening to the book for the last hour, determination to say something had welled up in me -- David was certainly not going to do it. And I'd just get more and more miserable. *Finally, the moment came.*

"One reason I'm disappointed that we weren't alone in Palm Springs is I was hoping we could go over the season and figure out what went well and what didn't and maybe come to some agreement on how we can improve," I said, my voice trembling a little toward the end.

"You mean you've been keeping that a secret from me the whole time we've been away? We could have talked plenty right here in the car! We've been together a whole week and there certainly has been time," he said, clearly unhappy.

"It's just that I think there are stressors to working together all the time and we have to face up to them," I said. "Your reaction is evidence in fact that you're as much at the end of your string as I am. I couldn't believe you told Michael we were happy as two peas in a pod."

"That's not what I said -- all I said was we found innkeeping fun. I am just curious to know what kind of 'stressors' and why have you waited until now to raise this? They can't be very important if you haven't raised them for nearly 1,500 miles."

At that moment, my cellphone rang. It was my niece Avery saying her mother, our sister-in-law, had died. While it wasn't unexpected, like all deaths, it was a shock. We talked through what had to be done right away, whom I would call, whom she would call and arrangements. Avery was understandably upset, so I stayed on with her in the hope that I could help calm her down. At some point during this time, I looked over at David and he was winding his finger in a circle, indicating I should get off the phone. When I didn't end the call, he tapped my knee and repeated the same move.

I turned my head away from David, toward my window, determined not to be interrupted.

"I'm so sorry we're not there with you, Avery. But let's stay in touch all day. We're going to be in the car, so it will be easy to reach us. Do you want to talk to Uncle David?"

I asked this because she is close to David and I was sure he could have a soothing effect on her. I looked over his way and he was shaking his head "no" vigorously and holding up his hand like he was a traffic policeman.

When I finally got off, I was furious and so was he.

"This is a good example of what I was talking about," I said. "How is it that you are the monitor of my cell phone usage? I was talking to our distraught niece about Walton. You still have your mom, so maybe you don't know how devastating it is to lose your mom. I do and that's why I think it's important. After all, it's only been a year since her dad died. She deserves airtime, for sure. But how come you're the decider?"

"I'm the one who pays the bills, that's why. There's no point running up our phone bill with needless calls. Do you know how much it costs?"

"Maybe we need to get a new plan if it's costing too much. These plans change all the time, I at least know that. I admit I only vaguely know what it costs and you know that. But I thought we were *partners* in the business and just because you're the one who pays the bills doesn't seem to me to be a good reason for you to be my overseer. That's not a partnership, in any sense of the word. I'm embarrassed and mad as hell that you do this kind of thing. If it's not about the phone, it's something at the Inn and you tell me in front of the staff or guests. This is *exactly* the type of thing I hoped we'd discuss." Whew. I was shaking.

"But you only told yourself you wanted to have this conversation, not me," he said. "That's not much of a partnership either, is it?"

"It sounds to me as if this conversation feels threatening to you. It sure is to me," I said.

"You need to accept that there are some things I know more about than you do, and respect me," he said.

"What? I can't believe you said that. Of course I respect you. I'm talking about you having respect for me!"

Silence. Lake Shasta went by. More mountains to go over, around and wind down. I pushed back tears, determined to stay strong. Silence. I couldn't think of anything but getting help.

"The only thought I've had at this point is that we need to find someone to see. A counselor. A marriage counselor, maybe," David said,

Now my eyes filled with tears, whether I wanted them or not. HE SUGGESTED IT and I couldn't quite believe it.

"Are you serious about getting marriage counseling?" I said.

"Sure. We have to do *something*. It sounds like neither of us is very happy the way things are right now."

I heaved a sigh that originated in my toes and exhaled a hoot louder than an owl in distress. "I don't know of anyone who does marriage counseling," I said. "But I'm sure we can find someone."

Back in Ashland, I asked a few close friends if they knew a marriage counselor. It was hard to do because somehow I was ashamed to admit we needed help. Especially since every one we knew thought we were the happiest couple in the world. John and Dot Fisher-Smith came highly recommended by the first two people I asked. Pillars of our community, these two wise older people welcomed us. They were quick to admit that they had no actual credentials as therapists, but they'd been working with couples for years. While it cost more than either of us expected and wasn't covered by our insurance, we agreed *we* were worth it.

Our first assignment was to make a list of all the things that had brought us together in the first place, all the things we loved about each other and what was really important to each of us as man and wife. Then we had to look each other straight in the eye and share our list.

"I never expected any one to love me as much as you do or to love anyone as much as I love you," I said.

"You have to say it again, Deedie, you looked down at the end," Dot instructed.

"David needs to hear what you believe," John said.

Blushing, I tried again. When I got to "love anyone as much as I love you," I started to cry. I grabbed David's hand, still looking into his bluer-than-blue eyes, now brimming with tears.

That was our foundation.

124

The best part of working with a couple was their ability to uncover simmering issues and guide us into facing them. If Dot sensed I wasn't participating enough, she'd ask for an explanation of why. If John saw David grimace, he'd want to know why. They both pointed out that some of the issues surfacing seemed to be less from working together and more from bad habits acquired over a long marriage. They said these needed "remediation."

The next week's assignment was even harder. Looking each other in the eye, say what makes you mad or sad with your partner.

David went first. I turned to face him squarely, nervous about what was coming.

"I think one of our problems is that Deedie doesn't listen to me."

Dot interrupted him. "Remember, David, this is something you're saying directly to her."

He started again, stuttering a little. "I don't think you pay enough attention to me, or listen to me," he said. "If you don't agree with something I say, you just do it your way."

"Is it fair that we always have to do it your way? Are you my boss?"

"No, but I'd like to be respected."

"I don't feel respected if I have to obey you," I said. David winced.

"It doesn't help that whenever something comes up, you just stop talking, drop out and ignore me," David said.

"Is that really what happens?" Dot asked me.

"I'm just not a good arguer, never have been. I guess it's the easy way out for me," I said. "My parents always argued and I hated it, hated it!"

"Remember when you're talking, you should be looking at David," John said. "Can you imagine for a moment how you'd feel if David became your *silent* partner? It sure would drive me crazy if Dot did that."

"I see, I see. I hear what you're saying. I guess it's a bad habit of mine," I said to David.

It took the rest of our session to come to an agreement that whenever we identified a situation, we'd have a "business meeting" to work out a standard operating procedure that would avoid whatever the point of conflict might be. We further agreed that business meetings would be for issues related to "the business" and personal issues would be dealt with in "home meetings."

When Dot and John asked what some of the personal issues might be, David complained that I seemed to be unenthusiastic about cooking dinner each night.

"Unenthusiastic is an understatement!" I said. "We both work at least 12-hour days and somehow it doesn't seem fair for me to always be the one who organizes dinner."

"You've always done it before," David said.

"Yes, I know. But things are different now and I think we should share the responsibility the way we share everything else," I said, now tearful. "I'm tired at the end of the day and I actually don't feel like eating or cooking."

"But dinner can be our relaxing time," David said.

"Not if I'm the only one responsible," I said.

Over the course of a year or so, we spent an hour a week at the Fisher-Smiths. Sometimes painful, occasionally joyful -- it was always work, but work we'd begun to look forward to.

"Try to remember that no matter what, love really does conquer all," Dot said.

The four of us were standing, our hands joined, at this, our last session of marriage counseling with Dot and John. "Let's each say it," John suggested. "Love *does* conquer all."

It sounded pretty trite after all the work we'd done trying to repair the damage four years of being in business together had done to our 40-year-old marriage, but that was indeed the lesson we'd learned. We walked up the their driveway hand in hand.

"I'm glad we did something about our issues, aren't you?" David asked, squeezing my hand.

"I'm *really* glad," I said, remembering how hard for us to even acknowledge we needed help. "It's hard though. Everyone always says how lucky we are. If only they knew the dark underbelly of our relationship."

"Every couple has a 'dark underbelly,' Deedie."

In the end, the belief that our love conquered all had become part of our DNA.

Until the dust-up over the sausages, less than 24 hours later.

I left the girls to finish the kitchen while I worked in the garden trying to focus on the notion of *love conquers all*. As I pulled the first few weeds from around the delphinium, it struck me that I was letting "all" conquer love by getting upset whenever there was a bump in David's and my road. If I let these weeds be all I saw, I'd never appreciate how beautiful my delphinium was.

Pretty soon the weed bucket was almost full and it was time to begin party preparations. As I was gathering up trowel, clippers, bucket and gloves, the Cuban ladies were coming up the driveway, each in a different day-glow color of flip flops.

"You guys somehow manage to make all of this look so easy." Carole said.

"We decided at lunch that it's practically unbelievable how you and David work together 24/7 and seem to always be going in the same direction, always getting along," Judy said. "Gus and I could never do that."

I jumped down the few feet from the raised garden. I'd heard the same thing from other guests before, but never during a period when I was feeling so raw about things between the two of us. I'd decided that remembering the delphinium, not the weeds was a good mantra for me this day *and* that I needed to lighten up. Use humor, as Dot and John had counseled.

"Tell you the truth, there *are* times when it just isn't easy at all. We've even had to get marriage counseling and I'm not embarrassed to say that." I looked around to see five faces suddenly in varying degrees of surprise verging on shock.

"I have to start getting ready for David's surprise party," I said.

I went into the office to print out the words to "When I'm 64" and found David getting ready to leave.

"Where are you going?" I asked, almost accusingly.

"To the Y, like I do every day at this time," he said.

"What? You can't miss teatime," I said, flustered, grabbing his arm. "It's your birthday. I bet the Y's closed," I sputtered, lying.

"It is not, and you know it," he said.

"But I want you to be back very soon. Promise? Really! It's important. Maybe you should drive rather than ride your bike." I said.

"It's a great afternoon for a ride. I'll be back. Don't worry."

"Please, please on time," I said, giving him a hug and a kiss. I could feel love beginning, ever so slowly, to conquer all.

"Okay. I got the message," he said breaking away. "What's going on anyway?"

"You just go and have a really good work out, okay?" I said.

I went back to the kitchen to finish putting olives, nuts, cheese and crackers and some fresh macaroons on plates and shifting them to the tables in the garden. We needed to get glasses and wine set up for the bar. Between all our guests and friends I'd invited, I figured about 30 people were coming. At the last minute, I'd run across the parking lot to pick up the birthday cake at the Safeway. Much as I didn't believe in store-bought cake, I simply couldn't squeeze one out of my busy day.

Don Marston, my friend the singer, walked up the driveway as I was lining up the glasses. "I hope you have an extension cord, because I forgot mine," he said, setting the piano down. "Gosh, this place is much bigger than I ever realized. You guys must work really hard."

"I'll get you a cord. And yes, we do work hard. But we have lots of help," I said.

I took one last look around the garden. All the hanging baskets. Most of the plants had been deadheaded and had lots more flowers coming. The pots of geraniums lent spots of color. Wisteria thick with creamy white blooms draped themselves over the door to Richard's room. Baby roses in profusion climbed the arbor the arched over the sidewalk down the driveway. Our dry stack garden wall shone in the late afternoon sunlight. *All our work over these years had paid off in beautiful scenes like this.*

Within minutes, people started coming from all directions. Our friends from the parking lot. Inn guests from the side entrance. Where was David? But then I reminded myself he would never boycott an event, no matter how irritated he'd been with me hours earlier. The Cuban clan had lined itself up against the garden wall. You could pick out the siblings easily, as most were short and a little stocky. Jim, Cristina's husband, stood out because he was well over six feet. I began to wonder if David had had a bike accident. *Why did my mind always zipline to the worst-case scenario?*

Musician Don was eager to get started, as he was on a tight schedule. Alissa passed among the guests with the song sheets. Just as I dialed David's cell phone to see where he was, I saw him coming up the driveway, right by my weeded garden. I signaled Don Marston to start the song.

"When I get older losing my hair, many years from now…" we sang as Don played.

I went to greet David, smiling broadly. He draped his arm around my shoulder, looking around at the assembled people.

129

"Will you still need me, will you still feed me, when I'm sixty-four?" Don Marston reached the end of one verse and riffed toward the second.

David squeezed my shoulder. I put my arm around his back and squeezed him.

I looked up at our musician. All of a sudden he seemed to be playing in slow motion. His eyes were glued on Judy, in the corner, back against the wall. Tall and blonde, standing next to her husband, Gus. Whatever was the matter? Had he forgotten the words? Thank heaven everyone kept on singing. I saw Judy take a few steps forward and put her glasses on.

"Send me a postcard, drop me a line, stating point of view..." Don Marston seemed mesmerized. His usual high energy and verve, gone.

As the song ended, Don Marston moved out from behind the piano, trance-like. He apologized immediately. "I'm sorry, Deedie. I know I flubbed, but I *think* that's my very first girlfriend over there. Is her name Judy? I haven't seen her for over 30 years!" he said, moving in slow motion toward her as if she were the only person in the garden that hot afternoon.

"It *is* you, Don Marston. I know you. I can't believe this," Judy was saying as she started toward him, her face suddenly in high flush. They embraced in a long hug, rocking back and forth a little bit.

"You know this guy well?" Gus was asking me.

"Pretty well. He's my choir director," I said. "Had you ever heard about him?" I asked.

"Oh, I probably have, but don't remember. What can I say? I know my wife's beautiful. They probably met in college or somewhere," he said, shaking his head. "But we all know first loves don't really ever go away."

Cristina came up with two glasses of wine. "Well, brother, this is remarkable. Don't you think we ought to toast them? You're not worried are you?"

"I'm not worried," Gus said. "I never worry about our love."

David came up to join our group. "So how'd you like your serenade?" Gus asked.

"I loved it. Just like I love Deedie. I'm 64 and I still need her," he said, putting both his arms around me.

"See what I told you. They get along *all the time*," Cristina said, smiling at us.

"Well, most the time," David said, squeezing me again.

"Yes, most the time," I said.

Judy and Don Marston were getting up from the table now. They hugged, lightly. She came over to our group, while Don left to pack up his sound system and piano.

"That sure was intense, almost magical," she said, taking Gus' wine glass out of his hand and sipping. Everyone smiled.

Don Marston approached us as he left. "Thanks for this phenomenal opportunity," he said, shaking his head and looking toward Judy. "I'd almost forgotten how good high school was. Wow. Bye Deedie, bye David. You have quite a place here. Sort of magical."

He hoisted the piano up on to his shoulder and walked back down the driveway singing, "When I get older, losing my hair…will you still be sending me a valentine…" louder and more confidently than he had the first time.

Anne Hathaway's Salsa Alegria

- ¾ c salsa (mild or medium)
- 1 cup chopped artichoke hearts
- ¼ c grated Parmesan cheese
- 1 c shredded Monterey Jack cheese
- 1 c shred Cheddar cheese
- 6 eggs
- 1 8-ounce carton sour cream

1. Grease a quiche dish and spread salsa over the bottom.
2. Sprinkle artichokes and Parmesan cheese over the salsa.
3. Top with the Monterey jack and Cheddar cheeses.
4. Combine eggs and sour cream in a blender and pour over the cheeses.
5. Bake 45 minutes at 350 degrees. Serves six to eight

Anne Hathaway's Wedding Chorale

Joy for the friends I've made, joy!
Iris, 4/07

I dug in my pocket for a hankie. Perspiration bathed my body; down my back, my legs, behind my ears. My watch nearly slid off due to my slimy wrist. I took cover under an old down elder tree in the large backyard of our Garden Suites.

"It's almost time to bring the bride across. Over." I called my husband, David. Our primitive cell phones had a walkie-talkie feature we'd found invaluable when we expanded our B&B operation to encompass the quaint set of cottages across the street from the original Inn in 2004.

"What bride are you talking about? Over." he said, sounding a little short. Maybe he was overheated too. He must've been unloading our black Ford F-150 after his weekly run to Medford. A week's worth of half-and-half, heavy cream, sausages, cheese, crackers, bacon, 25-pound bags of sugar, oatmeal and flour. How could he have forgotten?

"You remember, don't you? That woman who called the other day and wanted to spend her one-night honeymoon here? The one Pam referred to us? It's *tonight*. They're going to be *married* right over here in our garden in about *fifteen minutes*. Pam's already here to perform the service." I grabbed a quick breath, rushing to get the most information I could into a short broadcast. "The bride's waiting upstairs in the Hamnet room. You're the designated escort to bring her here. Over."

"Oh, right. Now I remember. The bride. Ooops. She's right here on the porch," he said. "You should see her. Over." I thought I could count on him. Creating events is a specialty of ours, wrought over many years together. Given some of the events we've pulled off, this one was relatively easy and uncomplicated. Except for the heat. And him forgetting, if even momentarily.

"Call me when you set out. I'm getting some music ready. Over."

"I'll finish unloading and be right there. Over."

Just a few days earlier, I'd been in the office working with Alissa, our manager, on the schedule for the next few weeks. Juggling the chart of room reservations with staff availability is a challenge, to say nothing of laundry, watering, sweeping, teatime, ironing and all the rest. And the phone kept ringing. Ring. A news release was needed for the Rotary Club's upcoming fundraiser and I was in charge of public relations. Ring. How much of a discount would we give if someone's sorority rented the whole inn for a weekend in September? A ding on the computer indicating a new email contained the news that a guest arriving that day was gluten-free.

"Alissa, could you go on-line to research some gluten-free recipes? This woman's staying five days." A current guest peeked in the door of the office. "Excuse me, but I left my key in my room and I'm locked out."

"Alissa, will you please get the master key and let her in? I'll keep working on the scheduling. Do you know where David is? He's in charge of keys."

Ring. Aaargh. This caller identified herself as Tracy and said she'd been referred to us by my friend, Pam Turner, a local judge. Non-stop and breathless, she told me that she, at 47, and her fiancé, 71, had decided they should get married so they could "sleep together."

"Uh-huh," I said.

"Even though we aren't kids anymore, we're old-fashioned that way," she said. "I was married before, but he's never been married. Can you imagine?"

"It's sweet," I said, forgoing the urge to tell her we'd been married almost 50 years.

"We're ranchers up here on the prairie. Both our families have been here for generations. We met at a bar not long ago. I'd heard about him and he'd heard about me. I think we might have even gone to the same church."

"That's great," I said, but I don't think she heard.

"Please don't get the idea we're bar rats. It was at a party for a mutual friend. Anyway, Judge Pam – I called her out of the Ashland phone book – she said she knew you. She suggested we get married and have our honeymoon, all at your B&B. Neither of us can afford to get away for more than a night. I got sixty head of cattle to worry about and he's got double that. Do you happen to have a vacancy on Wednesday night?"

The prospect of a wedding would be appealing to our guests, I instantly felt. It definitely was to me. The plays at the Oregon Shakespeare Festival were entertaining and inspiring, but this live theatre right here at the Inn would be a super bonus. From our phone conversation, I was getting the sense that Tracy was right out of Central Casting for older brides from the prairie.

"Perfect. Everything's falling into place. One more thing, if you don't mind. I happened to stop at my friend's bridal shop and she had a wedding dress in size 14, my size, reduced from 299 dollars to 99? Can you believe it?" She took another deep breath.

"The reason I'm telling you all this – 'hope it's not too boring – but I bought it because it makes me feel like a princess. Then when I called Roger – that's my fiancé – he told me *he'd* bought a new outfit, including new cowboy boots. Isn't that wonderful? Hello, are you still there?"

"I'm here, Tracy." I waved at David walking by, wondering where he was going, where he'd been.

Before our conversation ended, I'd learned that the ceremony would be at five, the bride and groom would get up extra early to do chores so they'd have plenty of time when they got here, and that none of their families were going to know of the wedding until it was over. Tracy was in an advanced state of wild anticipation, you could tell even if you didn't know her.

Practically as soon as our phone call ended, she called back.

"Hi, it's Tracy again. Whoops, one more thing. Is there a separate place where he could change while I'm getting ready in our room, so we won't see each other until the ceremony? I'm pretty traditional. Also, I might need help with my dress. It's a lot to handle. I was so pregnant when I got married the first time a wedding dress was completely out of the question."

Buzz. My walkie-talkie, David calling. I needed to get off. I hit the button that would tell David I was offline.

"Either the staff or I will be able to help. Don't worry, Tracy," I said.

This would be Anne Hathaway's third wedding. The very first wedding occurred on Halloween, an Edgar Allen Poe-themed ceremony. I performed the ceremony for the second one. Amelia and Dave, who had been coming to stay with us twice a year for ages, were thrilled when we got our young bagpiper friend Elias to play.

The morning of the cowboy wedding, after we'd finished serving breakfast, the staff and I met to brainstorm. David didn't have time to join us, as this was his bridge day and he wanted to be sure to get all the watering done before he had to leave. I was kind of surprised he was still going to bridge when we had a big event, but it was also provisioning day, so…I guess he decided he might as well make the trip to Medford for bridge and supplies.

Colleen and Camelia offered to decorate the tree under which the ceremony would take place. "We can use that white ribbon we have on hand for anniversaries," I said. Colleen volunteered to make a centerpiece and strew rose petals in the newlyweds' bed during the ceremony. I offered to get champagne and make "baby cakes." These tiny cupcakes with hearts iced on them used the carrot cake recipe for David's sister's wedding cake. I agreed to figure out the music. Meeting adjourned.

Around eleven, I was in the kitchen putting the fourth pan of baby cakes on the cooling rack when I heard a massive engine outside the window. The trash truck? But it was the wrong day.

I stepped outside to find a bright red truck so large it could barely squeeze into our driveway. The cab must have been four feet off the ground, gleaming chrome and spotless. A large wooden cross hung from the rearview, along with one of those green pine tree deodorizers. Tracy popped out of the passenger seat in white shorts and a low-slung jersey top. She was tall with lots and lots of blonde hair that must have been heavily sprayed into place. She hugged me into her amplitude.

"We're here! Cut the motor, sweetie," she said. She turned to close the door.

"We are so excited. We listened to Christian music the whole way down. Thank you so much for making this all possible."

The groom ambled around the back of the truck, his hand outstretched, ducking to avoid the rhododendron. He was every inch a cowboy – five-gallon hat, plaid snap-button shirt, weathered Levis, high cowboy boots, and a leathery, tanned face as wrinkled as an unironed napkin.

"Honor to meet you," he said, shaking my hand vigorously. This was the powerful hand that had milked a cow or two. Or wrangled a few bulls. Something. His bright brown eyes sparkled under the brim of his gigantic hat.

Once the bride and groom were oriented, I got to work with the pastry bag to ice the hearts on the baby cakes once they had cooled. The kitchen door rattled. Opening it, I found Tracy beaming, clutching a very small bouquet of one rose, some baby's breath and two ferns.

"Can you believe it? This wonderful man insisted I have a bridal bouquet. I told him he shouldn't spend the money, but he went ahead anyway. I told the florist girl to give me something as simple as possible. Isn't this beautiful?"

"It surely is. What a thoughtful man you're marrying," I said. "Colleen is making a boutonniere with a rose from the garden so the groom will have a flower also. Everyone here is as excited as you are," I said, turning back to work on my hearts. I could tell already this heart idea was going to be hell to implement. Not only was it so hot they were melting even in the air conditioning, but the creeping arthritis in my aging hands was making it a little painful to be squeezing so hard and so long.

"This is such a beautiful old house," Tracy went on. "I love being in it. Roger and I can't decide if we should live on my ranch or his, or find a totally different spot. He's up there getting his clothes together now. I'm so glad you have a place where he can wait until the ceremony because I really, really don't want him to see me in my gown before the wedding. My gown is hanging in the bathroom right now so the steam from the shower will get any wrinkles out."

"Shall we put the bouquet in the 'fridge so it doesn't wilt in this heat?"

"'Sounds good," she said, perching on the kitchen stool.

My hands were cramping from drawing the hearts of thick icing on to the cakes. Tracy sat there, looking out the window, quiet for the first time. I'd just finished the last cake when Roger appeared at the door carrying a clothes bag over his arm, a huge black Stetson dangling from his fingers by its chin string.

"Now it's time to hide him," Tracy said, jumping down to give her true love a quick kiss on the cheek. "I'm going upstairs to get ready," she said.

Alissa arrived to report that all was ready. "Would you accompany Roger and his duds to the Club House? And while you're there, please fill the champagne bucket with ice and put these bottles in to cool. I'll be over with the cakes in a few minutes. And please tell Camelia to come over as soon as she can to help the bride dress, okay?"

This was beginning to feel like it did when each of my children got married – so many details, but so much fun. Put teatime treats out for the guests in the house before the wedding. And remember to forward the main phone to my cell so we wouldn't miss any important calls, like new reservations. Change my shirt because this one had icing all over it. I still needed to find a CD with appropriate music for the wedding march on it. Could I get everything done on time? There wasn't a tray big enough for the dozens of baby cakes and those hearts were beginning to melt a little and we weren't even outside yet. I quickly covered a large cookie sheet with foil, lined up all the cakes and carefully balanced the whole tray between the baskets in the big deep freeze. I ducked into the powder room, the only room in the house not air-conditioned, and was instantly overwhelmed by the heat. *Everything* would melt, I feared, including me.

Ten minutes later, I lifted the improvised cake tray out of the freezer and made my way across the street to the Garden Suites. I'd found a wonderfully cool white eyelet blouse to wear that let the air in and my skin breathe. I patted my pocket to make sure my cell phone/walkie-talkie was there.

How great to see the transformation of the garden! White organza ribbons festooned the railings on the path between the cottages. In the back yard, two trees were wrapped in ribbon, bows blowing in the exceptionally warm breeze. The silver champagne bucket sat on a table in the little shade available there, surrounded by glasses. A big basket (it may have given prior service at Eastertime) contained Colleen's gorgeous flower arrangement bursting with roses, boxwood, gaura, daisies, snapdragons, zinnias, plus a few from our neighbors, sat next to it. The Garden Suite guests were out on their respective porches sipping their usual afternoon wine. Buzzing about the impending nuptials could be heard from every corner.

"Where's the groom?" I asked Colleen, who was taking the last of the dry sheets off the clothesline strung between the Club House and one of the cottages.

"In the Club House with Judge Pam," she said. "Wait 'til you see him. He's really dolled up." Hoping that a little time in the Club House 'fridge would help preserve the melting hearts, I opened the door to find Pam and the groom having an animated conversation. Colleen had not exaggerated. Roger was a vision in black and white. A big black hat with white piping threw a shadow on a starched white shirt piped in black. The skintight, creased black pants were held up by a silver buckle the size of a business envelope.

"Hi, Pam. Look at you, Roger. You are really done up!" I said.

"Not everyday a guy gets married." He stood up as he spoke. "I'm still in a state of wonder that a guy my age could find himself a beautiful wife like Tracy." Looking up, he said, "It's the hand of God. I know that for sure." He nodded up and down, then pushed his hat back, letting it drop. The hat strings, intertwined with silver, hung at his throat like an elegant necklace. This guy was sharp.

"Roger was asking if we could put some scripture into the ceremony, so that's what we're working on now." Pam said. "I think we have about another ten minutes, right?"

I looked at my watch. "Yup, that's about right. Do you need a Bible? David went shopping for provisions, but he should be ready shortly. I'm going to work on the music."

"I don't think we need a Bible and I didn't know anything about the music. Do I need to know?" Pam asked as I was closing the door.

"Yes. There'll be music. Wait 'til you hear," I said.

The solution to music had come to me as I crossed the street. Mounting the raised "dinner deck" so everyone would be able to see me from the surrounding garden and porches, I used my cheerleader voice.

"Welcome, welcome everyone." I said, standing on one of the teak benches. "As you already have heard, we're having a wedding this afternoon, and you're invited to be the witnesses. Since we need some appropriate music, I'm hereby recruiting you to do the job. Are you willing?" Everyone started chuckling. "When I give you the signal, you start singing the Wedding March, "Here Comes the Bride." You know, Dum, dum, de dum. Dum, dum, de dum. Da, da, de da-a dum." I felt like a seasoned choir director.

People began humming snippets.

"Okay, let's practice." By now, people were lining the edges of the porches. "You can stay up there in the choir loft or come down here and be a part of the congregation," I said. "C'mon now. Dum. Dum. De. Dum…." They all joined in enthusiastically. It sounded better than I'd thought.

My walkie talkie rang. "Deedie. I'm over here with the bride and we're starting across the street. Over." David rang off.I climbed down from the bench and headed for the Club House. "Pam, it's time you and Roger came out to stand under the tree," I called. "Everyone else, you wait for the signal. I'll keep my eye out for when the bride and her escort start down the path."

I positioned myself where I had a view of the path. People began gathering, wine glasses in hand. Everyone was smiling. Judge Pam and Roger did a stately walk across the ten yards from the Club House. Roger looked as nervous as Pam did placid. I couldn't imagine how hot she was under her long black robe, dripping as I was from every portal of my body.

There they were! David in his khaki shorts, Anne Hathaway polo shirt, and sandals, shirt made a shade darker by perspiration. The resplendent bride beamed on his arm. Three-tiers of pouffy bouffant skirt fell from a snug strapless lacey bodice. Holding tight to David's arm with one hand, clutching her modest bouquet with the other, she seemed to be swaying a little, giving the skirt momentum to do the same. Her spike white shoes that made her even with David at 6'3" clicked on the pavement. An organza hibiscus covered one side of her head, each stamen coated with sparkles. She and David smiled at each other as old friends or relatives would.

As they reached the head of the path, I called out in a stage whisper, "Okay, everyone. Strike up the chorus! Now!"

"Here Comes the Bride" rang out in dums and dahs and dees. I took my place and joined the slightly off-key cacophony. All eyes were riveted when the bride and groom caught sight of one another. Blackened by heavy mascara, a big tear rolled down Tracy's cheek. I found myself hoping she had Kleenex to catch it before black hit white.

David escorted the ecstatic bride to her place next to the ecstatic groom. As they turned and faced the judge, I was grateful that the ancient walnut tree behind the elder provided a thick canopy of shade. David moved over to the table where the champagne was cooling, prepared to pop the first cork as soon as the vows were spoken and the declaration of matrimony had been made.

Judge Pam opened the ceremony with Scripture, which she seemed to have magically produced:

Love is patient, love is kind. It does not envy, it does not boast, it is not proud. It does not dishonor others, it is not self-seeking, it is not easily angered, it keeps no record of wrongs. Love does not delight in evil but rejoices with the truth. It always protects, always trusts, always hopes, always perseveres. Love never fails.

Then she asked if there was anyone in the crowd willing to be a bridesmaid and hold Tracy's bouquet during the exchange of rings. A fifty-ish woman in yellow shorts and bare feet, blonde hair peeking out from under a floppy blue sun hat, stepped forward. Handing her wine glass to a friend, she stepped next to Tracy, who smiled and whispered, "Thanks."

The vows were simple and traditional. With Pam's help, Tracy went first, saying in a shaky voice: "I promise to be your loving and faithful wife," and grabbing Roger's hands when she got to "wife." Roger kept holding Tracy's hands tightly while Pam, patiently led him through the same vow, one word at a time.

"I now, with the power invested in me by the state of Oregon, proclaim you husband and wife and wish you a long and happy life together," Judge Pam said.

The first cork was being coaxed upward when the wedding guests suddenly broke into an impromptu version of Mendelssohn's wedding recessional.

"Dum, dum, de, dum, dum, dum, dum-de-dum, da-dum..." They'd barely gotten through the first few notes when the cork made an arc into the air, rising from David's position five feet away right and landing at the foot of the bride.

"Oh, this is just too, too much," Tracy said. Roger, somewhat closer to her height in his new boots, wrapped his arm protectively around her and fished a handkerchief out of his back pocket.

"We aren't used to this kind of attention," he said to the cluster of guests around them offering the couple best wishes. "I never would have dreamt it. I didn't know it was possible to be this happy." He steered Tracy toward the table that held the champagne and baby cakes. The hearts looked more like blobs at this point. The heat may have melted the hearts on the baby cakes, but the wedding melted a few other hearts in the meantime.

The husband of the bridesmaid came up to me during the reception to report his astonishment.

"I can't believe what I saw. I was napping, hear all the commotion, come out on the porch and the next thing I know I'm part of a wedding! It was better than a Fellini movie, ya know? Is this woman your relative?"

"'Just another guest," I said.

Tracy's Wedding Cake

- 4 eggs
- 1 1/2 C. salad oil
- 2 C. sugar
- 3 C. grated carrots
- 2 C. flour
- 1 tsp. baking soda
- ½ tsp. salt
- 1 C. chopped nuts
- ½ tsp. cinnamon
- 1 C. coconut
- 1 C. golden raisins puffed in water, then drained

Pre-heat oven to 350.

1. Mix all ingredients in large bowl.
2. Pour into 9x13 greased pan, bake 40 min. OR
3. Using small ladle, pour batter into miniature cupcake pan with liners and bake around 15 min. until firm on top.

Icing

1. Cream 1 stick of softened butter together with 8 oz. cream cheese.
2. Add approximately 1 box of confectioner's sugar.
3. Add 1 tsp. vanilla.

Optionally, add 1 C. nuts

Canine Therapy

Hattie is around to remind all of us that love is the greatest gift of all and she would like some now, please.
Judith, 9/02

Our new guest Mayo was standing at the threshold to the living room, ready to check in. Rushing in from the kitchen wiping sticky hands on my apron, I strode toward her. Our much beloved chocolate lab, Hattie, had gotten up off the sofa, wagging her tail, ready to give Mayo's hand her customary wet welcome kiss.

"I do not do dogs," Mayo said, her voice slightly raised, backing up a few steps and raising her hands up over her head, not even a hint of a smile.

I was taken aback. "Oh she's really quite friendly. Not to worry. Hattie, come over here," I said, sweetly, and then again with authority. Hattie responded by having another look at the guest and wandered my way, licked my hand and languidly climbed back up on the sofa. Every other guest had been delighted by this double welcome, often more interested in making friends with the dog than with me.

"I've been coming here for years and there's never been a dog in sight," Mayo said, without rancor, just informationally. "I think they may have had a cat. But I have to confess I was shocked to see that dog coming toward me. Is it always here? Going to be here the whole week I am? I don't mean to cause a problem, but…"

"I'm so sorry if you were frightened," I interrupted.

Apparently bad childhood experience had soured Mayo on dogs, I learned. Well into our third week of innkeeping, Hattie had proven until that moment to be an unexpected asset to our fledgling career. She greeted guests warmly and willingly, stayed out of their way unless they came looking for her, and was happy to help out by finishing up any left over sausage or breakfast food. She had quickly developed a knack for knowing just exactly when would be a good time to saunter out to the breakfast table in the garden to check for leftovers. If guests had taken their last bite, sated by their three-course breakfast, unable to put another morsel into their mouths – this was the moment every day when Hattie presented herself to the assembled. She'd dutifully stop by the side of each guest, eternally hopeful that some sharing of food was in the offing. Even though we counseled guests that her figure could really not afford any extra calories, she was the welcome recipient of daily surreptitious treats. Sometimes when she'd spied a particularly attractive bite left on a plate, she'd linger longer at the guest's side and was known to nudge elbows in the hope of seconds.

That evening, David and I discussed the fact that Mayo didn't "do" dogs. We decided it would be best if we tried to confine Hattie to our quarters, in the rear of the Inn. We simply couldn't take the risk of scaring a valued guest, particularly one who said she'd been coming to Anne Hathaway's for years and stayed a week in the spring and returned for a second week in the summer.

But then again, most of the other guests really relished having her.

"Just put her in our bedroom. We have to," David said.

"Mayo's staying for an entire week. It's not going to be easy," I said. "Hat's going to be lonely and the guests are going to miss her."

While Hattie was a social being whom by all appearances liked her new job, she quickly sensed that she was on Mayo's bad list and took it upon herself to make things right. This trait, with which many dogs and cats seem to have been hard-wired, manifested itself immediately after we instituted the quarantine. Whenever she got free of her bedroom prison because we forgot to shut the door tightly, she headed directly for Mayo as if she were a homing pigeon. Mayo firmly spurned these efforts, explaining to other guests that she had an aversion to dogs and repeating her story.

Another guest named Greta took it upon *herself* to counsel Mayo about her fear of dogs, telling her she knew others who had overcome bad childhood experiences. It was possible, but of course Mayo would have to be willing.

"Really, there's research that shows dogs are good for you," I heard Greta say to Mayo the next afternoon. Seated across from each other in our comfy wicker chairs on the front porch, I couldn't help seeing and hearing everything on the porch because my office window is right there. I'd noticed that Mayo was spending a good bit of her time out there, safely out of Hattie's free roaming range. "They release dopamine in your brain, and that's the stuff that makes you feel good," Greta continued.

"I don't mean to be disrespectful, but I really do look forward to coming to Ashland for the plays," Mayo responded. "I teach Shakespeare – and I'm not sure I want to fit Dog Therapy into my schedule. I'm already pretty busy," I heard Mayo respond, throwing back her head, and with it her long black locks, smiling respectfully.

"How about if we just get Hattie out here and you see for yourself how much pleasure it gives me to spend time with her?" Greta persisted, nodding her head vigorously, as if to encourage a positive response.

"I think it's time for the hike I always take before the matinee," Mayo said, getting up.

Greta came in and stood in the doorway to the office. "I just wanted you to know that I'm trying to get Mayo over her dog phobia. I'm a therapist and it's clear to me she'd be better off with some dogs around."

"You're great to want to help her, but I really think we have the whole thing under control," I said. "Hattie seems to have gotten used to being shut up for now. I think it's better we leave it this way, if you don't mind," I said.

Just as I finished my sentence, David came to the door. He had been eavesdropping from the living room, just a few steps away from the office. "We really need to let her be, I think," he said to both of us. "Making a big deal out of it is just going to make the problem worse. We don't want to lose a guest over it."

"That's what I was just saying to Greta," I said tentatively, now not wanting offend *her.*

Greta shook her head slightly, maybe grimaced a little. "Whatever you all say. You're the owners. I could bet you she's out there on her hike thinking about what I said, though. She's very, very bright."

"Thanks for your help on this," David said to Greta, heading back to the living room and *The New York Times.*

"So, do you specialize in any particular kind of therapy, Greta?" I asked.

On day three of Mayo's visit and Hattie's involuntary imprisonment, I was once again putting out teatime treats. Today the sweet was Currant Events and they were in a big pan on the cooling rack. A tasty bar of stewed currants spread between rich crusts of butter and oats, I loved using my old friend Judith Bird's recipe on Wednesdays because they reminded me of grammar school when you had to have a news clipping to read on Wednesday. And currants were a surprising and unusual ingredient anyway.

As I was carrying in the nuts and some crudites, guests named Tom and Louise were suddenly there.

"Can we have a word with you?" Louise asked.

"Sure, but let me bring the cheese and crackers and Currant Events out first," I replied.

"We just wanted to tell you how much we miss having Hattie around," Louise began. "She's so sweet and she helps us not miss our Sadie, who had to stay at home. Sort of dog therapy, you know? We heard from Greta you were keeping her away from guests. Any chance you'd reconsider?"

"We played with her in the garden yesterday and had so much fun," Tom added.

"The problem is, we have a guest who has a real aversion to dogs, and for good reason. She'll tell you about it if you ask. We decided it was just best to keep Hattie in the back of the house so she wouldn't bother that guest. Maybe we could establish visiting hours for Hattie." The minute the words were out of my mouth, I worried that our bed was unmade and the room untidy.

"Yes, Mayo already told us about her 'dog issue' and we've been talking to her some about it," Louise said. "And we think she's making progress. Maybe today during tea we could bring Hattie out and *maybe* if Mayo sees how much the rest of us like Hattie and think she's great, she'll give her a try."

Argggh. It felt like the entire house had decided to change Mayo's attitude toward dogs. This seemed unfair to Mayo, and all of a sudden I felt like I needed to save her from them. But I didn't want to alienate the dog lovers either. Here she was on her vacation and here we are rookie innkeepers with a dog that she's *rightly* afraid of. This was a much more challenging situation than discussing why the Oregon Shakespeare Festival had chosen to do *Macbeth* in modern clothing. We had to figure out a way to politely discourage the group therapy approach that seemed to be emerging.

I was concerned also because I was certain David was going to be upset when he got wind of this latest strategy. After all, one of the reasons we'd come here in the first place was so we could be inspired by the theatre and all the interesting people it attracted. Dogs! Well, we loved them, but we were certainly willing to recognize there were those who didn't share our sentiment. And after all, we couldn't impose our dog on people, especially if they'd had a trauma in the past. We weren't in the dog therapy business. We were innkeepers.

This had become a recurring theme for us – recognizing where we had a role and where we didn't. No, our job was not to do dog therapy. No, our job was not to help a staff member get over being jilted by her boyfriend. No, our job was not to get the man next door to cut his hedge like ours. Much as we'd like to be able to do all of the above, we had enough to do becoming the best innkeepers we could be.

Hattie remained in our room at tea time.

"Why is Hattie out in the living room?" David asked, coming into the kitchen where I was laying out the next day's implements so they'd be ready when I returned to the kitchen at 6:30 a.m.

"By popular demand. First it was Greta, then Tom and Louise. Then they got the Brodericks to ask too. They're all convinced they can change Mayo's mind about dogs in general and Hattie in particular and they promised to keep her under their control so she wouldn't go near Mayo."

"It sounds like we're going to lose Mayo as a guest before this is all over. Four years she's been coming here – that's the kind of business we need and want to build on. Everyone's told us that and it was in that one book we read about owning a B&B. I think we're taking a big risk," he said, looking more serious innkeeper than loving husband.

Damn! Here I was doing something wrong again – at least wrong in his eyes. He definitely had a point. But everyone was so positive about it, and I'd seen Mayo's eyes when she looked at Hattie when I'd let her loose at tea time. She wasn't immediately repulsed by her the way she had been the first day. I shook my head, trying to shake out my negative feeling.

"You may be right, but I saw how it was going once Mayo came back from the theatre and it seemed like things were headed in the right direction. Really, I'm not kidding," I said, tiptoeing up to him with a kiss for his cheek. Kissing was always a good cure for me and maybe it would work in this instance on my business partner.

He smiled, patting my shoulder. "Let's keep a close eye on it, though. I'm going out there to see what's happening, monitor the situation."

"I'm just going to hope for the best is what I'm going to do," I said.

Around dinnertime, I thought all the guests had pretty much cleared out, off to the theatre. This was the best part of being innkeepers in a theatre town – once six o'clock rolls around, the Inn empties out. I poured myself my usual glass of wine and went to look for Hattie. I hadn't seen her since tea time and had been so busy getting everything ready for breakfast, I hadn't even thought about her. David had said he was going to the Y after checking on the dog situation. But where was she? Not in our room. Not in the yard.

I went out to the front porch, afraid that someone had let her out and I was going to have to spend my usual decompression time hunting the neighborhood for her. And there she was. Having tea with Greta and, of all people, Mayo!

"There you are, you naughty dog! Come on, you come back inside right now," I scolded, looking at Mayo in as apologetic a way was as I could muster.

To my surprise, Mayo spoke next. "Oh, don't take her away. Greta and I were just having a great time visiting with her. I've actually found Hattie and I have a lot in common. She's really quite sweet and very polite. How old is she?"

"Wow!" That was all I could say.

"Well Wow! for me too," she responded. "We were just sitting out here chatting while Greta was patting her, and I found myself wanting to pat her also. That's how it all came about. Can you believe it? I can't." Mayo was shaking her head.

I looked Greta's way and she was winking as hard as she could, and even though there was a big blonde curl hanging down over her left eye I could see it.

The next day – the day before Mayo was scheduled to leave -- I was in the office preparing invoices for all the people who would be checking out in the morning. I looked up and there was Mayo. At first she didn't say anything.

"What can I help you with?" I asked.

"I have an unusual request. And I don't want you to be concerned if you can't fulfill it," she said. "But as you saw yesterday afternoon, Hattie and I have developed a relationship, maybe even a friendship. I was wondering if you ever let her have a sleep-over."

"A sleep-over? You mean you want her to sleep in your room with you?" I asked, incredulous.

"Yes, that's what I mean. Greta was absolutely right. She makes me feel really good and I was just thinking that maybe I'd sleep better with her in my room. I have a new job and it's been keeping me awake at night. I was thinking maybe that sense of calm I got when I was petting her might help me sleep."

I paused a moment to think of the implications of the Inn's dog becoming a sleep enhancer and decided to say, "Sure, if that's what you'd like."

Hattie arrived in the kitchen not long after we did the next morning, wagging her tail and smiling. Right behind her was Mayo. "Shall I take her for a walk?" she asked.

"It's probably best if I do that," David said. "She has a tendency to take off after cats or deer and I wouldn't want her to pull you down. But thank you so much."

"Did you two have a good overnight?" I asked.

"She is really good company, you know," Mayo said. "I read my book and patted her head for awhile and then she just curled up next to the bed and went to sleep for the whole night. Did you know she snores sometimes?"

"Yeah, I think she has dreams," I said. "Thanks for having her. I'll get her to write a little bread and butter note later."

When Hattie died several years later, our regular guests slowly but surely heard about her passing. The first sympathy card we received came from Mayo. Shortly thereafter, we expanded our property to include cottages just across the street. Mayo was the first to suggest it would be a perfect setting for guests' dogs. We took her up on her suggestion and ever since our guests have been sleeping well – with their own dogs.

Currant Events

Judith Bird

- 1 1/2 cups sifted all-purpose flour
- 1/2 teas salt
- 3/4 cup brown sugar
- 1 cup rolled oats
- 2/3 cup butter or margarine
- 1/2 cup chopped nuts

Prepare and cool currant filling

Filling:

Combine 1 T cornstarch, 1/2 teas cinnamon, 1/4 cup sugar, and pinch of salt in saucepan.

Add 1 cup of water, stir until smooth.

Add 1 1/2 cup currants, which have been rinsed and drained.

Bring to boil over low heat stirring frequently. Then cook 5 minutes.

Remove from heat; add 1 teas lemon rind and 1 T lemon juice

1. Combine flour, salt, brown sugar, and oats in large bowl.

2. Cut in butter until mixture is crumbly.

3. Firmly pat half of mixture into bottom of greased 9 x 13 pan

4. Spread with filling. Combine nuts with remaining crumbs, sprinkle over filling. Pat down well.

5. Bake at 350 degrees for 30 to 35 minutes or until golden brown.

Olivia and Her Friends

That was so thoughtful of you to buy the kids all sunglasses.
It helped when we took them out for walks.
— Richard, 10/03

I didn't expect to find pigs in their room.

We'd become instant friends with Kathleen and Nancy when they checked in. Maybe it was because the first thing they said was what a breath of fresh air we were compared to the former, very terse and business-like owners.

Anyway, the weather had turned cold and dreary that first October we were in Ashland. They'd complained they didn't bring warm enough clothes to wear to the outdoor Elizabethan theatre and were very worried they'd freeze. I figured I could help them out. They looked about my size. So, using the master key to get in their room, I'd put some wool slacks and sweaters on their bed while they were out to dinner.

It's always hard for me not to feel a little like a snoop when I go in guest rooms when they're not there. I especially try not to notice medicines or take note of clothes strewn sloppily this way and that or drawers half closed or what they're reading. But it was absolutely impossible not to see that this room was overrun with pigs! The most stuffed pigs I'd seen this side of FAO Schwarz. I recognized Olivia from the children's books I'd read to my children. But why would *they* have them? These pig owners had to be close to 60. The largest and prettiest porcine, outfitted in a pink velvet dress, hat, sunglasses and Mary Jane's, appeared to be overseeing the situation from the dresser. Another few were napping on one of the beds. I peeked in the bathroom and couldn't help noticing that a small piglet in Greek sailor garb straddled the Kleenex box, a vision in navy cap and a striped shirt, an Olivia flashlight chained to his hoof.

In the kitchen the next morning during breakfast preparation, I asked Colleen if she knew anything about the pigs, figuring she would remember because these two women had been coming to the inn for several years before we took it over.

"Oh, they're regulars," Colleen said.

"The women or the pigs?" I asked.

"All of them. It started with just one and every year a few more get added," Colleen said. "I usually re-arrange them when I go in to make their beds. Then we all laugh about it. They're school librarians. They told me it all started because Nancy had a collection of pigs in her library that her students kept adding to. Now that she's retired, the tradition has shifted. Now it's between the two of them."

"It sounds to me as if we'd better think up something particularly pig-gish to do today," I said, delighted to now be in the pig loop.

"I was thinking it would be good to arrange them as if they were having a tea party," Colleen said. "I think they'd really like to have tea like everyone else does in the afternoon. Don't you?"

"That seems like the only hospitable thing to do," I said, all business. "I'm pretty sure that slight sow in the velvet dress has been to England and knows a cup of tea when she sees one."

When I went out into the garden to chat with the guests after breakfast, Kathleen and Nancy were regaling everyone with what an amazing inn-keeper I was for being so thoughtful to provide them warm clothes to wear to the outdoor theatre.

"I just got back from Arizona, where it was so hot I couldn't stand it, so it didn't even occur to me to pack winter clothes," Kathleen was saying. "It's not many inns you can go to where they provide this kind of wardrobe assistance, but I tell you I was toasty warm last night, thanks to you, Deedie."

"They weren't even in *my* colors," Nancy said, laughing. "But they sure worked. Thank you so much."

"Well it's also pretty unusual when guests come bearing pigs," I added.

"*Pigs?*" the other guests asked.

Before long, everyone knew the story of how the pig collection had started. First there had been just a few. Then on a trip to Ashland, Kathleen bought Nancy an Olivia doll for the collection, then Olivia got lonely and wanted a friend and on it went from there.

"Why don't we ever get to see them?" our guest Bill Wilson asked. "I'm going to think this is all hogwash unless we get to see them."

"Well, think about it," Nancy said. "How would you feel if you were Olivia and you were surrounded by people eating bacon and sausage?"

"We try to be sensitive and compassionate," Kathleen said with a perfectly straight face. "Bacon for them is *almost* worse than the prospect of pig prostate trouble."

As Colleen left the kitchen to go make beds and tidy up rooms, I decided it was high time to surprise Nancy and Kathleen with a public debut for these pretty pigs of theirs. Returning from the matinee that afternoon, our guests were greeted with the usual tea table laden with good things to eat – Irma Heck's oatmeal cookies, fresh strawberries and cream, almonds and a wheel of brie with crackers. On a small side table in one corner of the room was a piglet-sized tea table with small chairs from the toy box we have for visiting children. Seated at the table were four of the visiting pigs. A tiny bouquet of flowers sat in the middle of the table and in front of each pig was a miniscule morsel of an oatmeal cookie and one cashew. Four demitasse cups we'd gotten as wedding presents for their tea completed the pastoral pig tea.

I was in the office on the phone taking a reservation when Nancy and Kathleen stopped in on the way to the dining room, carrying a new baby piglet.

"Just for you," Nancy whispered, putting it on my desk.

I nodded and waved, trying to concentrate on the reservation and smile at the same time. Just as I was saying good-bye to our future guest, I heard whoops of laughter from the dining room as the auxiliary tea table was discovered.

"Oh my heavens. Oatmeal cookies are Olivia's absolute favorite," Nancy exclaimed.

"How ever, ever did you know?" Kathleen asked.

Other guests seemed a little taken aback and then someone exclaimed, "Oh, it's Olivia and her friends!" An older, very grandfatherly guest interrupted, saying, "I haven't heard the name 'Olivia' since my grandmother died in 1943. It's such a beautiful name, I sort of hate for a pig to have it. She was such a grand lady. One of the first women to graduate from Stanford Medical School," he reminisced.

"Wow. She must have been quite a trailblazer," Warren said, slicing some of the brie to make a cracker sandwich. Then, turning to Nancy he asked, "How do your girls feel about brie? Could I cut them each a small piece?"

"Olivia's lactose-intolerant," Kathleen said quicker than a gnat can blink. "Don't give her any or we'll have hell to pay. A gassy pig is no fun at all, believe me."

The whole room erupted.

"How ever did you discover *that* connection?" Claudia asked in mock seriousness. "My daughter is and it took us years to figure out what the problem was."

"Easy," said Nancy. "She farted all the time whenever we gave her milk to drink."

"Did everyone love the production of *The Tempest*?" David asked when he returned home from his bridge game after teatime.

"I'm afraid we never got to discussing the play this afternoon," I said, laughing to myself. "We had a tempest of pigs in a teapot!"

"What?" he asked.

"Today's conversation was all about *pigs*. Do you remember how much Lucy and Sara loved the story of Olivia the pig and her friends? You must have read it to one of them."

"Not really," he said. "Whatever does that have to do with Shakespeare? It sounds pretty silly to me." Hmmm, I thought. David needs to lighten up some, or maybe I need to get more serious. For me, the whole thing was hilarious, a welcome break from the steep learning curve we'd been on for these first four months of our career as innkeepers.

"Really, honey, it's hilarious. Kathleen and Nancy have all these pigs they bring every year. They even have a journal the pigs have kept of each visit to Ashland."

"I'll take your word for it," David finally said, going back to his newspaper. "But one thing I think you need to keep in check is your enthusiasm for these things. Our guests are not here for pig games and might find all this tiresome, don't you think?"

Keep my enthusiasm in check! I was furious.

"You seem to be the only one finding it tiresome so far," I said. I went into the office to Google pigs in Shakespeare so I could prove that the revelry going on under our roof was not only fun, but probably relevant!

Alas, there's only one mention of a pig in the whole canon and people have wondered out loud why he was so pig-aversive. I told David at dinner what I'd found out and that he might consider that we were filling the pig gap for our guests. He was not nearly as amused (nor enthusiastic) as I was.

When we got to the Inn at 6:30 the next morning, the tea table was in a state of dismal disarray. We customarily leave all the teatime food out for guests returning from the theatre hungry, so there's always stuff to clean up. But this morning, things looked like a ship wreck. The port and sherry decanters had been moved from their spot on the side serving table and now dominated the center of the table. Tipsy-looking stuffed pigs, large and small hovered nearby. Olivia's dress was half off, her brother's glasses were on top of the port bottle, Nick the baby was sitting in the middle of the brie plate and Oliver was leaning precariously against the Waterford sherry decanter.

A veritable porkloin bacchanal…hog heaven!

David was finally amused and began laughing quietly, shaking his head as he picked up plates and port glasses. We smiled at each other across the table. As I carefully dismantled the elaborate display, I struggled not to laugh out loud and waken the guests asleep in adjacent rooms.

Starting in on the day's scones, ideas for our next pig step occurred nearly as often as I added another ingredient. It came to me that we should have a *piganza* celebration. Speaking quietly, I asked David to help. Sort of like Kwanzaa, but for pigs only.

"We have to do something good, because today's their last day," I said.

"You do the scones, I'll manage the swine," he suggested, getting our recipe notebook down from its shelf.

Scones in the oven, I got the blackboard to write down the day's menu. This was the time each morning when I always asked David what we'd be having for meat, as meat is always his department.

"We can't have bacon," I whispered. "It gives the pig crowd indigestion."

"I think we should go ahead and have pork and when they ask where the pigs are, we'll just tell them they're eating peanut butter in the kitchen. Our pigs on the farm always loved peanut butter," David said.

"You're kidding, aren't you?" I asked.

"Nope. They loved it. I remember smearing it on corn cobs for them. It was great for fattening them up for market."

"Good morning, folks. We were wondering who absconded with our pigs," Kathleen asked, opening the door from the dining room.

"Oh, don't worry," David said. "They're on a field trip, but I think they'll be back in time for breakfast."

David was finally totally on board! Hooray, I thought.

While we were putting the finishing touches on breakfast, Colleen filled the wagon we use to transport things between the Inn and cottages across the street with our herd of swine. We were sure they must have had hangovers, but they looked happy and delighted with the gigantic peanut butter jar in their midst.

Everyone had gathered in the garden for breakfast wearing jackets. The air was a little chilly so we'd turned on the outdoor heater. The gentleman with the grandmother named Olivia was the first to ask after our guest, Olivia. I told him Olivia would be here shortly and just as I finished saying that, Colleen arrived pulling the wagon full of party pigs.

Everyone cheered. "I want to meet this Olivia," our older friend said, getting up to greet them.

Three days later, a thank you note arrived from Olivia, saying she'd be back next year. "Your hospitality was genuinely overwhelming," Olivia wrote. "William oinked most the way home and we think it's because he didn't want to leave Ashland."

Fourteen years later, Olivia and her now thirteen friends take up much more space. Kathleen and Nancy have switched to a larger room.

When Nancy called to reserve a larger room in the cottages, she said, "The kids were feeling really crowded and not enjoying themselves as much this last visit. Olivia even wrote in her journal about it. We do still plan to come across the street to the Inn for breakfast, though."

"That sounds like a good plan. What about the kids' breakfast?" I asked.

"They'll have the continental breakfast in the Club House next to our cottage, and maybe come for tea once or twice," she said. "That way, they won't have to confront the bacon factor at the B&B. I told them there'd be no meat at all at their breakfast. They'll love the hard-boiled eggs. "

"Great. We can have Vivienne's Sausage Roll while you're here without feeling guilty," I said.

"Oh, super. I'll tell Olivia and she'll be relieved," Nancy said.

Vivienne's Sausage Roll

- 3lbs. bulk sage sausage
- 2 bunches chopped scallions
- 3 lbs. mushrooms, sliced thin.
- 1 tbsp Worcestershire sauce
- 1 tbsp Tabasco sauce
- 1 tbsp dried thyme
- salt and freshly ground black pepper
- ready-made puff pastry
- butter

Preheat to 400

1. In large skillet, brown sausage. Transfer to large bowl
2. In same skillet, fry onions and mushrooms until just dry. Add to bowl and mix in Worcestershire, tabasco and thyme. Add to sausage and mix.
3. Roll the puff pastry out into a large rectangle, then cut into two long rectangles.
4. Place a layer of sausage meat mixture down the middle of each pastry rectangle, then brush each with beaten egg on one edge.
5. Fold the other side of the pastry over onto the egg-washed edge. Press down to seal and trim any excess. Cut each pastry roll into 8-10 small sausage rolls.

Place the sausage rolls onto a baking tray and transfer to the oven to bake for 15-20 minutes, or until crisp and golden and the sausage meat is completely cooked through.

Rooms at the Inn?

"We're home," they called from the rear door upon
returning for their seventh visit.
Mark Antony Suite, 8/10

I'd heard about Innkeeper's Insomnia, but never experienced it as badly
as I did two nights before my birthday in 2009. Checking to see who
would be coming the next day just before bed, I discovered I'd only reserved
four rooms for a Berkeley group that always needed five. This would be
their sixth visit – they were the kind of "repeaters" innkeepers love for their
steadfast loyalty. And I didn't have room for them.

Before turning in, I'd called all over town to see if *anyone* had a room.
Nope. Not even the Motel 6 (that's just how desperate I was). Well, to be
honest, I didn't call The Dark Forest Night Inn. They rent by the hour and
I just didn't think it would work for the Berkeleyites. In mid-August, we
hardly know what day it is. No time between check-outs and check-ins to
come up for air. It's the same for every lodging establishment in our town.
The 3,000 theatre tickets being sold for each day's performances belong to
people who need a place to sleep.

To make matters a little worse, David was away taking care of his mom,
so this problem, caused by *my* oversight was on *my* shoulders alone. As
I turned off the light, I told myself and maybe God also that it would be
heavenly if I could wake up with the solution to this predicament.

I lay completely still on my back, exhausted but so enervated my legs couldn't settle down. I'd bend my knees. Then straighten out one leg, then the other. My legs were on automatic pilot. I was out of control physically, if not mentally. *Maybe I could get the staff to clean our condo and put them here in our house. I could easily sleep at a friend's.* No, too much work. The condo's too messy, if not filthy. Slovenly for sure. We may keep everything at the inn pristine, but somehow our living quarters are never a priority. Ah! Turning on my side, I remembered our neighbor Tim saying we could use his condo if we ever had any overflow. He would be away for the entire summer. Maybe that would work. Back on my back, I tried to recall who was scheduled to work the next morning. Would we have enough help to make Tim's condo into an Anne Hathaway's satellite? I had mentioned it to Alissa, but never any details. Sitting up for a minute to trick my body, I worried what the guests would think if we shunted them across the street. Besides, I'd never even been inside Tim's place, though I knew David had. Tim was a former San Diego policeman and author of mysteries that usually involved a significant amount of blood. Who knew what his taste was, even though he was an expert on Shakespeare? Maybe I should switch some other guest, someone new. I began to imagine the Trip Advisor entry appearing in my mind as I turned to my left side, where I never sleep.

We made our reservation in January for four days in August. Nothing could have prepared us for being sent to a neighboring condo instead of staying in the beautiful Garden Suites across the street. While gracious, the innkeeper really wasn't able to provide a satisfactory explanation as to why we were relegated to this house, which she referred to as the Antony and Cleopatra Suite. It was just this side of tacky.

Maybe the right side would be better. While I wanted to keep my eyes closed in case sleep came, I opened them long enough to see it was 3:03. Oh God. Only three more hours to get any rest. I began counting, something I hadn't done since the night before my college finals. I decided to try to count how many scones I'd made so far that summer to put myself to sleep. I kept losing track of the numbers, forgetting how many people we had when, then starting over....at some point, maybe it was 107 or so, I began to drift. Thankfully.

Dragging myself to the kitchen the next morning late, at 6:30, I told our manager Alissa about the problem and my solution that sounded even better when I said it out loud. *Maybe I wasn't as stupid as the insomniac of the prior night, I wondered.*

"We already cleaned Tim's place the other day, so it's usable. Didn't David tell you before he left? He said he'd talked to Tim and he thought we ought to do it. I can't believe he didn't tell you before he left. It just needs towels and soap," she said. "Just what are we going to call our 'new' room?" she asked.

"Huh! I can't believe he didn't tell me either -- I might have slept better last night. As for the name, 'hadn't thought of that, but Tim the owner says he'd name it 'Antony and Cleopatra'. What do you think?" I decided not to tell her I'd already gotten an advance copy of a Trip Advisor entry about it during my endless night. For some reason, being confident around staff seemed a better choice than sharing my frantic sleep-free nights. "Did you know I've probably already made more than 200 scones this season?"

I was patting down the fifth round of cranberry orange scones, mentally adding up the number of guests versus the number of pastries we'd need that morning.

"Antony and Cleopatra *Suite,* I think," I said.

"That's good," Alissa said from the other end of the kitchen, where she was slicing melon.

BRIiiiiing.

Darn! The phone always rings just as I'm rushing to get something into or out of the oven. Alissa took the tray of scones from me and put them in the oven.

Good morning, it's Anne Hathaway's. Can I help you? I answered.

"Deedie, this is just a heads up," Dirk, the leader of the Berkeley five-room group, said. "Ted had a stroke yesterday, so of course, he won't be with us."

"How great!" I said into the receiver, which was covered with scone dough from my hands.

"Poor Ted. We're really concerned about him. I don't know if he's going to make it."

"Wow. So I guess it's for sure he can't come," I said.

"Deedie, of course he can't come. Maybe you didn't hear right. He is in critical condition."

"Oh, my, of course, Dirk. How absolutely terrible," I said. "I'm so sorry. With the radio on, I must have misheard what you were saying. Do please tell him and Charlise how sorry we are. We'll hope for the best recovery possible. And the rest of you, have a very safe journey up." Hanging up, I felt relief rain down upon me, inside and out. No need to displace *any* of our guests.

"Sounds like we won't be needing the A&C Suite after all," I told Alissa. "It's literally a *stroke* of good luck for us, but don't tell anyone I said that."

"You're bad," she said. "The scones are done. Shall I get them, or can you?"

"I'll get 'em. And let's not tell David that I told Dirk it was great that Ted had had a stroke, okay?"

Beginning now to feel guilty, I was sure that the healthy members of the group now en route were chatting among themselves about their ditsy innkeeper who thought it was great one of their long-time friends was hovering near death. *Maybe I'm losing it. Maybe this is a sign I need to start pulling back from innkeeping. My leftover thoughts from the bout with insomnia flooded back. There's just so much to worry about in this job and as much as I worry, I still screw up. I make hundreds of scones. Pull hundreds of weeds and everything's usually beautiful, except when I tell guests it's great that their friend is at death's door because it solves my problem. Maybe I should put flowers in their rooms just as a nice gesture.* Taking a deep breath, I decided there was no time to dwell on a problem already solved.

It was Farmers' Market Day. Gathering up all the empty berry crates and replacing them with full ones was something I always looked forward to. That, and selecting flowers for the arrangements in the living room and dining room.

I pulled our big F-150 black truck into the driveway to load up. Our big truck, which was practically a member of the staff it worked so hard, was David's most favorite piece of equipment. I found it intimidating to drive when he was away. For the first few years, our station wagon worked perfectly well. Then David was inspired to give me a surprise for my birthday -- a perky *little* VW bug convertible. The day after that, he announced at breakfast that he thought we had to get a truck, as the bug wasn't big enough to do all our hauling. While David had never been known as a schemer, suspicions ran high regarding this deal. He'd always wanted a truck and I was glad he finally had one.

The local Armory, just a mile or so down Main Street from the Inn, serves as venue for the Growers and Crafters market. It's a carnival-like scene with everything from five kinds of kale to pastries and eggs and Indonesian food and fresh starts plus too many gluten free and vegan products to mention. We have a regular route we follow each week, followed by general wandering.

"Wow! I'm so excited to have blueberries again, and raspberries too," I said, bubbling over with the delight of a gourmand to Cathy at the Pennington Farms booth.

"Do you have a lot of guests this week?" she asked.

"Almost *too* many," I confided.

"When does that threesome come? The one that always buys a case of jam? I want to be ready for them this year." she asked.

She was referring to Dean and Ron, who always come with Susan, bearing wonderful wine from their vineyard and various other treats for my birthday. Susan's priceless petit point Christmas ornaments made just for us overwhelmed us.

"You know, I'm really not sure. It's always around my birthday, which is day after tomorrow," I said, trying at the same time to visualize the reservation calendar, a huge spreadsheet with all sixteen rooms and the dates on it. When *were* they coming? I made a mental note to look when I got home. Funny I hadn't noticed it when I was poring over the schedule the night before. *Ohmygod. Have I screwed up again? They always come for my birthday. They always come for market day.* My pores felt like they were suddenly swollen with panic. I scratched my arm reflexively.

"Maybe we'll see them next week, then," Cathy said.

"Yup, maybe next week," I said.

"Happy Birthday, Deedie," Cathy said, placing a rhubarb tart (my favorite) gently on the berry box. Somehow my concerns about my waistline disappeared whenever I got a pastry gift from Cathy.

Back in the kitchen I unloaded all of our market fare into our industrial-strength refrigerator. No matter how much bigger this 'fridge is than our last one, a total re-arrangement is always necessary on market day. Four flats of berries – black, raspberry, blueberry and strawberries. Plus our weekly Community Supported Agriculture (CSA) box of produce. Even though there was room on the bottom, that had to be reserved just for meats and eggs, so the health inspector says. Once I was finally done, my knees sore from kneeling on the hard kitchen floor, it was time for my favorite job of the week – creating beautiful flower arrangements. I laid them all out on the counter and considered whether the lisianthus and dahlias would be compatible with the gladiolas and salvia.

The tall lavender glads stood naturally in the back of the Lenox urns for either end of the sideboard. Pink dahlias filled in nicely, circled by the purple lisianthus and dark blue salvia. I liked the blend. Yes, they'll be fine with the dark green boxwood as a contrast.

The other side of my mind tried to remember what the new arrivals liked best for tea, the next thing on my agenda. I permitted myself a millisecond to appreciate our efforts we do to keep guests feeling special. Then I remembered I hadn't checked on Susan, Ron and Dean's arrival yet. Drat.

I'd just put a stick of butter and four squares of chocolate in the microwave to make some Nutty Clusters when I looked up to *see* them. Susan, Ron and Dean! What? I was sure they weren't on the schedule. How could I have screwed up *twice* on the same day? Face flushing, I pushed my hair back – and stared at them.

"Here we are, back with you again, Kukla, Fran and Ollie, too" the threesome sang.

"How'd you like our song? We practiced the whole way up," Dean said. "We're so excited to see the new rooms. Are we actually going to be the first occupants?"

That's right. They wanted to be the first ones to stay in the new rooms. And I forgot.

"Is everything okay, Deedie? You look like you're in a state of shock," Susan said.

I was stuttering now. "Because you're such good friends, I have to tell you some very bad news," I said.

"What's happened? Is David okay? Where's Cappy, our favorite dog?"

By now they'd all stepped down into the kitchen and Susan had approached me with a hug.

"Everyone's fine, really, really. It's just that….to be honest, we weren't expecting you and we have absolutely no room at all and I was just about to check and see when you were coming and actually there are no rooms in town to be had and I just cannot begin to tell you how bad I feel." My mind raced faster than my tongue. I was now near tears as I spilled out the tale of woe I *thought* Ted's stroke had corrected. All my good feelings evaporated into the warm air the oven was generating for the clusters.

"Don't you remember? We said we wanted to be among the first to try the new rooms you were going to build. Did you not build them?"

"Yes, we did. But I'm afraid – really all I can think of – is that maybe the folder where I had the advance reservations was misplaced. This is just awful, and it's the second time, I confess, that it's happened *today*!"

My walkie-talkie rang. It was Alissa. "The Antony and Cleopatra suite is ready; we've been over it with a fine-tooth comb," she said. "I'll leave it open so you can see it. Over."

Our unexpected trio of guests had moved to the dining room, where I found them whispering among themselves.

"You aren't going to believe this," I said into the walkie-talkie, "But I'm on my way down there right now with the suite's first three guests. Over."

I looked up to find Ron, Dean and Susan lined up in a row, looking at me expectantly, leaning on the counter.

"So, I gather we have a room after all," Susan said hopefully.

"You are *so* treasured and *so* special," I said, "you're getting an entire condo, just like the one we live in down the street. You'll be our neighbors. Not a block away. It has two bedrooms and I can guarantee you're going to *feel* like you're in the Bard's embrace, really."

"This sounds like an adventure," Dean said, putting his arm around my shoulder as we moved through the inn.

"It just became available today," I said. "Just in time for you. You'll be its very first guests. I really hope you'll forgive me for screwing up. I know you're not going to like it as much as staying in the new rooms, but of course you'll come here for breakfast and have all the other advantages of the inn…tea time included!"

Now I remembered. I'd been interviewing thatchers for the roof when they were here last. Our architect was doing research on daub and board construction. The bank had enthusiastically endorsed the idea and given us nearly every penny in the proposed budget. We'd gotten all the permits we needed from the city and had a contractor ready to go. But, it was 2008, an unlikely time to be building because the housing market and economy were in free fall. David and I had lost sleep over whether or not we should go ahead. At 2 a.m. one early January morning, we discovered we were both awake and on the same page -- we needed to put a stop to this project or we might be facing financial ruin. We both slept well the rest of the night. The next morning, we walked together up the street to begin work on serving breakfast. As we passed the Garden Suites, we heard the sound of large machinery coming from the back alley. David went to check to see what was going on. It turned out the City had begun work on digging the necessary new water and sewer lines for our project, per the requirements of our permits. We, the innkeepers, said, "Hmm. Guess we're going forward with the project after all." We knew this wasn't the perfect model of corporate decision making, but that is actually how it happened. And how the file with the names of those who wanted first dibs on the new place got lost -- it was lost in our shuffle of inefficiency.

Walking down the block with them and their luggage, my mind raced. What would this turn of events mean for tea, for breakfast? I began toting up the numbers. When I got to 28, I decided to just worry about *today* and deal with *tomorrow* tomorrow.

Susan reassured me over and over again. "Deedie. Don't fret. This is just another delightful chapter in the Adventures of Anne Hathaway. Don't you remember when the oven gave out and you had to rush next door to use your neighbor's? We'll have a perfectly good roof over our heads."

"We never lack for drama," I said, shaking my head. "Here we are. C'mon into the Antony and Cleopatra Suite. Have a look around."

Ron went upstairs immediately with his suitcase. Susan said she had to use the bathroom and was glad to find there were two. Dean just couldn't stop laughing.

"This is a treasure," he said, looking around the darkened living room, surrounded by busts of Julius Caesar, Pericles and William Shakespeare, each with its own stand. "Do you think we could get this guy to give us some decorating advice for our flat in San Francisco? He really knows how to do it up, doesn't he?" he asked, giggling.

The custom-made headboard in the master bedroom bore the heads of Antony and Cleopatra on either side. We found Ron stretched out on the satiny pure polyester burgundy bedspread, leaving the Cleopatra side for Dean.

"No rolling Susan up in this rug," I said, pointing to the thick furry carpet on the left side of the bed.

"Not a chance," Susan said, joining us. "My rug rolling days are over."

We all laughed.

"Isn't this perfect?" I said, barely able to contain my delight that they seemed delighted. "I'm so relieved you're willing to be the first guests in the Antony and Cleopatra suite. Settle in and c'mon back up the street for tea at four," I said.

The phone was ringing as I returned to the kitchen. It was David.

"Everything going well?" he asked.

"Oh yes, very smoothly," I said.

"You sound a little harried," he said. "Don't worry, you'll get it done on time. Sorry I'm not there to help. Remember, don't fret over the small stuff."

As I lifted the nutty clusters from the cookie sheet, I heard people gathering in the dining room. I overheard the Antony and Cleopatra threesome introduce themselves as staying in our 'newest suite.'

As I arranged the nutty clusters on a silver wedding present platter with a lacy doily I couldn't help thinking 'nutty' was very much the way I was feeling. I opened the door into the dining room and announced I had nutty clusters made by the nutty innkeeper.

Everyone laughed. Dean interrupted to say he had something important to ask.

"What's that?" I asked.

"Can we reserve Antony and Cleopatra for next year? We *love* it."

Nutty Clusters

- 2 unsweetened chocolate squares
- 1/2 cup butter, softened
- 1 cup sugar
- 1 egg
- 1/3 cup buttermilk
- 1 teaspoon vanilla 1 3/4 cups flour
- 1/2 teaspoon baking soda
- 1 cup salted nuts, coarsely chopped
- Chocolate icing
- 2 unsweetened chocolate squares
- 2 tablespoons butter
- 2 cups powdered sugar

1. Preheat oven to 400 degrees.
2. Melt chocolate in top of double boiler over hot, not boiling water. Remove from heat. Cool.
3. Cream butter and sugar in large bowl until smooth.
4. Beat in egg, melted chocolate, buttermilk and vanilla.
5. Stir in flour, soda and nuts.
6. Drop dough onto cookie sheet. Bake at 400 deg. for 8-10 minutes.
7. Remove from cookie sheet to a wire rack. Frost while still warm.
8. Melt chocolate and butter in small saucepan over low heat, stirring until completely melted.
9. Add powdered sugar and water, mixing until smooth.
10. Yield: 3 1/2 -4 doz. cookies.

Tea and Sympathy

*I thought that maybe Anne Hathaway's ghost might let me
in to the secret of who really wrote her husband's plays. Alas,
I slept so soundly that if she came, I didn't hear her.
Will's Study, 3/12*

Claire's call for multiple rooms for multiple nights early in March – our shoulder season – wafted over a transom eager for traffic.

This first call from a Jane Austen group punctuated a dark January day when the huge grid that covers the entire computer screen with all sixteen of our rooms had begun to fill up, but not enough to ease the pre-season jitters entirely. Sitting in my yellow (the paint can calls it rutabaga) office at this time of year before the first plays open, I stay reasonably busy with one thing or another related to innkeeping. Checking emails for incoming reservations. Sending confirmations. Looking at who we're expecting and when. What rooms are still available. I try to scout areas where we might have a double booking or have reserved two rooms when the group wanted three. These are steps I've learned – sometimes painfully – to avoid last-minute surprises. And then there's hatching marketing schemes based on the season's plays.

Busily Googling The Jane Austen Society as Claire talked, I quickly learned that *Pride and Prejudice* being done at OSF was the draw. Using it as a marketing ploy had not even occurred to me because I didn't even know there were such things as Jane Austen clubs.

"A few of us have been to Ashland before, but we decided at our last meeting we couldn't miss something by Jane, so we're coming as a group," she said matter-of-factly.

"How great that you found us!" I said.

"We were attracted by the name of your Inn, I admit, " she said. "Another famous woman. We've been meeting for at least sixteen and a half years, maybe sixteen and two thirds. And it's definitely one of the most sterling features of my life."

"Really?" I said.

"Yes, ma'am," she said. "We throw ourselves into every word Jane Austen wrote and shut out the rest of the world," she continued, and then continued some more. "We've found all kinds of connections and parallels between our own lives and hers. Even though we live in different times. We have wonderful teas. You wouldn't believe how much she still has to teach all of us."

"How many rooms do you think you will you need?" I asked when she stopped for a breath.

"Four! That should do it. Can you accommodate us?" she said, "Yes, four."

"You want four rooms?" I said, trying to sound as casual as I could but not completely able to conceal my delight. "Let me see if we have four rooms available for those dates." I knew full well we did, but for some reason I always like to make it sound as if we're busier than we are even in advance of the summer high season. "Oh, yes, we do. Wonderful. You're the first Jane Austen Book Club to reserve with us." The English major in me was trying mightily to think of some Austen titles besides *Pride and Prejudice* so I could sound smarter and more knowledgeable. Quick, let me Google.

"We all want separate rooms," Claire went on, as I noiselessly Googled. "All but one of us is married, but our husbands won't be coming. Even so, we don't share rooms. Our husbands are just not interested. I mean, they're not interested in Jane Austen. And also, the group is the Jane Austen *Society*, not book group. It's actually international in scope."

"How lucky for us that we'll have some real experts sitting around the table. I'm sure other guests will benefit from your knowledge," I said.

"We can't really begin to be thought of as experts," Claire, who also revealed she'd been president of the group for the last five years ("And counting"), said. "But we do have our opinions and we aren't shy about sharing them. Maybe that's what drew us to Jane Austen or *what* our association with Jane Austen has done to us," she said, laughing.

"I remember trying to write something sensible about *"Ode to Pity"* when I was a freshman English major," I said (thanks to Google).

"Hmm. How interesting," Claire said.

A week before the group was due to arrive, Claire called again.

"Is this Anne? Oh, no. I know better. It's Deedie, I nearly forgot. I'm calling with news. None of us can believe this, but now our husbands want to come. They don't even know each other and we can't imagine why they want to come. It's the middle of the week, after all. So, would you possibly have enough rooms suitable for four couples, now, plus the single?"

"Do the husbands need extra rooms, or will the wives be sharing with them?" I asked.

"Oh yes, we'll share our rooms with them. And breakfasts. But they'll have to find their own entertainment," Claire said. "We've already informed them."

When I told David we were going to have Jane Austen spouses as well and he'd better be prepared to be their guide, he said he was ready.

With three Jane Austen groups already booked -- or Janeites as I'd seen them referred to on the Sacramento, California organization's website – we were more excited than usual on opening night in February of *Pride and*

Prejudice. We needed to orient ourselves. This was its first adaptation as a play.

Early in our innkeeping career, we determined that going to all the plays when they open is part of our job description. How else can we engage in intelligent conversation with our guests or advise those who ask for guidance on what to see? We'd made it a tradition to put His and Hers reviews of each play on our website once we see them.

As we were getting dressed, I tried to get David interested in dressing in Regency style, something Janeites know a lot about apparently. Should I wear a bonnet, carry a *reticulate*? How about a silk ascot for him? He declined, uninterested in my silliness. But as we walked to the theatre, we recalled our visit to the Jane Austen exhibit at the Morgan Library in New York just a few months before.

"What I remember is how strongly she represents the time she lived in," David said. "I'm looking forward to our guests and understanding how all these women have developed such an allegiance to her. I wonder if any men belong to the Jane Austen Society."

"Don't know, for sure. I can assure you none of Claire's group are men. All I can think of is what a prisoner of her times Jane Austen was. Compared to her, we're all so liberated now, we feel sorry for those who weren't," I said. "But you're right – it will be interesting to hear what they find so compelling about her."

As I sat through the play, it was hard to imagine how the Austen aficionados would receive it. They seemed so serious about the important literary tides running through everything she wrote. How would they react to The Festival's interpretation, which took a lighter look at the subject and had us laughing about prejudice and rejoicing in pride? What would they think?

President Claire and the members of the Jane Austen Society of Puget Sound burst into the living room like a new tide on the Thames. The husbands obediently followed single file in formation behind them. As the men fanned out to the fringes of the room in a semi-circle, each had the look of someone who wished he were somewhere else. President Claire was quick to impart two important facts about the husbands: 1. They had no interest in Jane Austen. 2. The only thing they had in common was a wife who was a member of the Jane Austen Society. While the women chattered among themselves about which room would be best for whom, the men remained silent, shifting from one foot to the other, interacting minimally. One lifted off his Seattle Mariners baseball cap and made a task of folding it several times so it could be tucked neatly into his back pocket, origami-like.

Why on earth did they come, I wondered.

"You play golf?" Sid, who was tall and slim, asked Norm, the hat tucker.

"Nope. No Jane Austen. No golf," Norm replied, locking his arms to his waist.

"I hear there are some good hiking trails around here. Maybe we men could take a hike," Dick said, picking up the slimmest thread of enthusiastic conversation and pushing his longish blonde hair back from his face.

"Now there's the best idea I've heard in a long time," Rosey said. And then, pausing after each word, she added, "The. Men. Can. Take. A. Hike."

"Rosey! We'll have none of that. Let's be good to these gentlemen of ours," Claire said. "Men, we know you can take good care of yourselves and you know we love you, but we're here to be distracted by our dear Jane Austen. But you knew that on the front end, right?"

"Yes, I think we all knew it, didn't we?" Sid said, turning to the others. Heads nodded.

Once everyone was settled in their rooms, they returned to the dining room for tea. A dispute broke out about what kind of tea Miss Austen preferred.

"I'm nearly sure it was black tea, always. And of course with the milk. Always with the milk. That goes without saying," Claire said.

I slipped back into the kitchen to get the milk. It was rarely requested unless we had a Brit in the house. By the time I returned, Rosey was coming right back at Claire with a correction.

"Have you forgotten that she was plagued with stomach problems? Dyspepsia, I believe it was. I feel rather certain she wouldn't have been permitted anything but a staunch herbal such as chamomile. Really. Think about it. What do the rest of you think?" she added, a little breathless. Rosey was what our family calls a sturdy woman. Both her appearance and her speech carried weight. Wow, these Austen fans were serious, I thought.

The men, meanwhile, had filled their tea plates with lemon bars, almonds, olives, sharp Stilton cheese and crackers. One had found the port bottle and carried the tiny glass and loaded plate in one big hand. None had tea, herbal or black.

We'd invited two of the young actors from the play to breakfast the morning after we knew the Austenites were seeing *Pride and Prejudice*. We couldn't help thinking our guests would love meeting them and the actors would get a kick out of their extreme devotion to the author who wrote the book on which their play was based.

"You're kidding," our actor friend Janis said when I extended the invitation. "They do nothing but read Jane Austen all the time? I feel like that's what I've been doing for the last six months, but I can't imagine a worse sentence than doing it for life. I had trouble getting through *Mansfield Park* once, let alone multiple times. Being knee deep in Jane Austen for the run of the play is plenty enough for me."

"Don't worry. You'll enjoy them, I'm sure," I said. "And they're looking forward to meeting professional actors."

The two actors, Janis and Kate, turned up a little early on the appointed morning. Getting them coffee in the kitchen, David gave a warning: "They're armed with a multitude of questions. I hope you're prepared.

They're incredibly knowledgeable about the minutest of details when it comes to *Pride and Prejudice*."

"This sounds like fun," Kate said.

"Their husbands are here also, but we seated them in the living room so they could talk about whatever they wanted and not be dragged into the P&P conversation," David continued his briefing. "They went to the play also, but I don't think they're nearly as engaged, shall we say, as their wives are," he added.

"David's going to stay with the husbands and I'll be with you two, the women and two other couples who also saw the play in the dining room," I said. "I have the feeling this is going to be a more interesting breakfast than usual. Good luck helping those poor men, David. They look like pathetic little sheep following after the women."

Opening the oven to take the scones out, I added, "One of them just confided in me that, unlike his wife, he'd never had a scone before coming here and guess what, he's discovered he rather likes them!"

"I'll come talk to them too, if you want me to," Kate said.

"Let's play it by ear," David said.

After breakfast was served, David and I emerged from the kitchen to take up our assigned spots in the two rooms. Chat 'Em Up time. I glanced toward the men and couldn't help comparing the volume of talk going on: Dining room, 10+; Living room, 0. David's job promised to be a lot more challenging than mine, I suspected.

"It must be awfully hard to play one of these roles when all you know about *Pride and Prejudice* is the script or the book," Claire was saying to Kate as I sat down.

"Actually, we do quite a bit of research, each of us does," Kate said. "Myself, I've read nearly all of Jane Austen's works. It helps that I was an English major at Swarthmore College. And as a cast, we learn quite a bit from the dramaturge who works with us. But we certainly don't know as much as all of you do. You've been at it much longer than we have," she added in a respectful tone, nodding her curly, curly head.

Talks in both rooms went on longer than anticipated, longer in fact than most any other morning at the Inn that year. When we re-grouped in the kitchen with our actor guests, David was pleased to report that the first Anne Hathaway's Self-Help Group had been launched at his table.

"It was truly amazing," he said. "I sat down and started asking these guys what they did for a living, just like you always do. And the next thing I knew, they were all telling me, in one way or another, they didn't have jobs! One was 'in between jobs,' another was 'reinventing himself' and the other two were laid off. I've been unemployed myself, so I know that wasn't easy."

"That's why they could come in the middle of the week!" I exclaimed.

"And none of them knew this about the other. One's a boat broker who says no one can afford to buy boats anymore. Another one's a wedding photographer who hasn't done a wedding in a year. Les was laid off from his job at Boeing because they didn't get some big contract and I forget what the other one does – or did," David rattled off the list in the reporto-rial style of his past as a newspaperman. "I found myself telling them about my own unemployment experience. I told them that's how we ended up as innkeepers," he said.

"So they came to breakfast believing the only thing they had in com-mon was their wives' membership in the Jane Austen group? And went away having discovered they had something very major in their lives in common?" I asked.

"Yup. That's right. And they all live within thirty miles of each other. They decided to have lunch together today after they go for a hike in the park," David said. "They'd already begun to get ideas for each other before they left the table," he added. "I told them they should keep on getting together when they get home. It really helps."

"Amazing. Does this happen all the time?" Janis asked.

"Never something like this," David said. "Instant support groups are not on our list of amenities. 'Seems as if the wedding photographer may get a job from the one whose daughter's getting married this summer," he added, smiling with pride.

Claire was the first to reach the tea table on this, the Jane Austen Book Club's third and final day at the Inn. It seemed unfair to me that anyone as thin as she could make more than one round of the calorie-laden table, and still be a perfect size four. Today she couldn't contain her enthusiasm.

"Audrey, come right away. You're just not going to believe this. We have the fresh strawberries with – I guess – *somewhat* clotted cream and there are these gooey chocolate bars that simply melt in your mouth. I've already had one and there's another on my plate."

Audrey, the only blonde among the Austenites, and the others appeared from three different directions, having been beckoned by their leader. "What are they called? I've never seen anything that looked remotely like them," Suzanne declared, carefully putting two bars on her plate. Her face seemed perpetually flushed, as if she was just in from a run.

I was busy filling the ice bucket at the bar. "Lemonade's ready now," I said, turning back to the table. "We call those Tea and Sympathy bars. My friend Lee Neff made them up. Aren't they scrumptious?" As I spoke, I couldn't help noticing a splotch of the runny chocolate from them on the starched white tablecloth. *Oh, woe, I said to myself. Chocolate stain. Never easy. I'd have to be sure to treat it once everyone left for the theatre.*

Actually, I'd re-named Lee Neff's bars on the fly. They are a perennial favorite we used to call Turtle Bars. But to reflect the victory of this visit I thought Tea and Sympathy Bars would be appropriate. The first strawberries were in, so out they went in the special, very British, bowl with the pitcher on one side for cream and a bowl on the other for powdered sugar. A nicely-aged brie and cashews rounded out the menu for what I called "tea" but had been corrected by one Austen expert who said it was more commonly called "Fourses."

The Austenites all sat around the table with their full plates discussing *Pride and Prejudice*. They weren't at all sure they liked this version -- "I don't think they realized it is really a *serious* piece," Claire said.

"I wonder where the men have gotten to," Suzanne wondered out loud. "I haven't seen my husband since breakfast."

"Oh my heavens, I'd nearly forgotten them," Audrey exclaimed.

At that moment, the front door opened and the men arrived in a group, talking animatedly among themselves about the movie they'd just seen.

"There you are!" Claire said. "You went to a movie? Really? Listen, girls…the men went to a movie!"

Everyone began to chatter at once as the men began helping themselves to the day's offerings. The port drinker from the first day poured a glass for each of the others and delivered them in person, nodding to each new friend as he handed them one.

"Were you all together?" Rosey asked.

"We sure were," Les said. "We've had a great day. We've made ourselves into a group!"

"Let's have a toast to that," Stan said, raising his glass of port.

"Hear, hear," Claire said, squeezing Suzanne's upper arm.

Tea and Sympathy Bars

From Lee Neff

Crust:
- 2 C flour
- 1 C firmly packed brown sugar
- ½ C butter
- *Caramel:*
- 2/3 C butter
- ½ C firmly packed light brown sugar
- 1 C pecan halves or pieces
- 1 C or so chocolate chips

1. Preheat oven to 350.
2. Put crust ingredients in Cuisinart and mix thoroughly
3. Pat firmly into ungreased 9x13 pan.
4. Sprinkle pecans over unbaked crust.
5. Cook caramel over medium heat, stirring constantly. Let boil 1-1.5 minutes.
6. Pour evenly over crust. Bake for 18-22 mins until caramel is bubbly.
7. Remove from oven. Immediately sprinkle with chips. Allow them to melt slightly, then swirl with spatula. Cool. (If you're in a hurry, throw in freezer for 10-15 min

The Case of the Missing Necklace

The knock on the kitchen door startled us both. I jerked up, unable to imagine who might disturb our peace at 7 a.m. The coffee was already out, so it couldn't be someone looking for their first cup.

Reaching up the two steps to open the door to the dining room, I spied the recipe for Pineapple Upside Down Muffins I'd been looking all over for -- in the "safe place" behind the Cuisinart. Phew, now I could get on with muffin making, but first I had to determine what was the matter with Sylvana Mark, who stood before me looking quite agitated.

"I've been robbed by a member of your staff," she said. Thin, evenly tanned with longish dark hair streaked in platinum, she stepped down into the kitchen and leaned against the counter where I'd been working.

It is definitely not customary for a guest to join us in the kitchen, but especially not during breakfast prep. We were in High Breakfast mode. I'd been looking all over for that recipe, wasting precious preparation time. David was making our signature home-squeezed orange juice using the ancient squeezer our daughter-in-law had recently claimed in the basement of the café where she worked.

This is a time of day we both love, silently going about our very familiar routines before any other staff arrive. Morning karma, we call it. National Public Radio's *Morning Edition* plays quietly in the background. We're always excited when Will Shortz comes on with the weekly puzzle and love to play along (I'm a tiny bit quicker than David is). We keep our pot banging, our voices as low as possible. This was our third and final day with the Markses and their friends. Problems arose almost as soon as they arrived. She was disappointed that we couldn't provide our usual full breakfast at 6:30 a.m. in order to accommodate an early tee time on the golf course. That afternoon, she wanted to know just which thing was gluten-free on the tea table, as she *sometimes* liked a gluten-free snack and our website said we could do that if necessary.

I leaned against the opposing counter so I could address her face-to-face.

"Oh my heavens. What's missing?" I asked. "How perfectly awful."

"Awful is right. A very expensive and beautiful necklace is gone. The one I was wearing when I arrived. I got it on our last trip to Santa Fe. We go there every year and I always buy a piece of fine jewelry. And I must say you had absolutely no right sending your staff into my room when I wasn't here." Looking first at David, then back at me, she said, "That necklace was in my room and now it's not, and your staff made an unauthorized entrance. You don't have to be a detective to figure it out."

This was uncharted territory, and ordinarily it would have put me into nervous mode. but there was something about Sylvana Mark that made me calm as can be. I'd already decided she had been sent to test and torture us on every front -- if it wasn't needing breakfast before the crack of dawn, it was coming down with a sudden gluten intolerance, or letting me know there were some crumbs on the sofa or telling me we shouldn't let our chocolate lab roam freely. A calm, professional, determined demeanor overtook me.

"I'm so sorry. This is something we've never had happen. And while I appreciate you must be very concerned, it would really be best for us if we could save the conversation until after breakfast. As you can imagine, this is the busiest part of our day. Would that be possible?" My voice was quiet and determined. I moved back to my baking post and starting stirring.

"No it would not," she said. Now she was *planted* against the counter, one ankle crossed over the other.

David put an orange half in the squeezer, then said, "I'm sure you'll find your necklace. And if you don't, I'm sure we will. We are always sending misplaced items back to guests."

While they talked, I shifted my eyes between Sylvana, the muffin mix, David and the recipe. The muffins were due out to guests no later than eight.

"Why don't you at least give me the names of the staff members who were on duty yesterday so I can talk to them about this when they arrive?" she asked.

"I'm afraid that won't be possible," I said, surprising myself with my firmness. "And by the way, unless you had the 'Do Not Disturb' sign on your door, we *expect* the staff to go into every room every day to make the bed, empty the waste baskets and tidy up. It's their job, and part of the routine here and at most other inns as well. I had no idea you did not want anyone going into your room." I moved back to my post and began putting pineapple and brown sugar in the muffin tins. *No use mentioning that this policy and lots of other information is plainly stated in the Welcome Book.*

"We'll talk later, but I'm not at all satisfied with your response to this," she said, glaring as she passed by me to depart.

I recalled my first conversation with this guest, months earlier. She'd called, full of questions. A quiet room upstairs with lots of sunshine would be best for her. Were the pillows soft or hard? Down or synthetic? What about the linens – cotton? Organic? Where did we get them, thread count? What kinds of things grew in the garden just outside her window? I'd even sent her several sample breakfast menus before she made a final decision. What kind of coffee did we serve? What time? Were there *always* scones, or did we ever make muffins?

At some point, she tripped my "question" wire – years of innkeeping have taught me that a barrage of questions on the frontend will likely lead to an overly demanding guest. That said, three rooms for three nights before the crowds arrive was a big piece of business. As I replayed my experience with Sylvana Mark, I decided it was time to start letting instincts rather than greed be my guide. Saying, "I'm sorry we don't have availability," when I see trouble on the horizon was probably a better way to go.

"So what do you think?" I said to David as soon as Sylvana Mark closed the door.

"I think we've got a big problem and need a strategy," he said.

"I've just been kicking myself for taking the booking in the first place. I knew. *I knew.* And I know exactly what that necklace looks like. It's one of those you see in museum gift shops and fancy art galleries in places like Santa Fe -- a tangle of polished rocks, turquoise and other semi-precious baubles. It looked as if it weighed a pound and a half!"

I scooped the batter into the tins and put them in the oven, then moved to the rear of the kitchen, closer to David.

"I think our approach should be be cool and professional in the face of all her drama, don't you agree? The only thing I am even slightly, *slightly* worried about is that the person who cleaned her room just started working for us."

Could it be that in spite of all the glowing references given by her former employers, she was a thief? My internal compass immediately pointed to No! After all, she worked for two of our good friends, and before that she worked at Oregon Shakespeare Festival in the costume shop. They couldn't believe she quit. She has a Master's degree. I was feeling sure.

"You mean it was Elise?" he whispered.

"Yes, but I have no worries whatsoever that she stole anything. Absolutely none," I said, standing close to his ear to be sure only he could hear. "And we should tell her after that if her valuable necklace doesn't turn up by tomorrow morning, we'll contact our insurance carrier and if they ask us to, we'll notify the police. Very straight forward. What do you think?" I took a step back and looked up.

David grimaced a little. "I agree. And since you're the one who's been dealing with her all along, I think you should be our spokesperson. Okay?"

"Fine. I'll tell the staff to refer her to me if she approaches any of them."

While the muffins baked, I began the daily search for the perfect color combination in a tablecloth. Fourteen for breakfast meant it had to be very large for the table, which would need all five leaves. I lugged them out of their space in the bathroom closet. I'd been putting these leaves into this table and taking them out again since I was big enough to lift them

I tried not to notice that Sylvana Mark was pacing the living room. Her husband and half a dozen other guests were reading the papers and chatting quietly. To my dismay, she came into the dining room when she saw me. "Can I give you any help?" she asked, a few strands of platinum hair falling over her left eye, her bronze top straying off one shoulder, revealing a red bra strap.

"No, thanks. I've been doing this for years. And the staff will be here soon to finish up."

"We really need to talk about the *theft*," she said. "I've been thinking how really attached I was to that necklace. And I'm not sure if I mentioned that it's very valuable. I'll be interested in talking to your staff when they get here." I put a table leaf back against the sideboard and went over to the doorway of the living room where she stood. "Come here, a minute," I asked, beckoning her into the dining room with me. She followed, adjusting two huge silver cuff bracelets, one on either arm. She stopped so close to me I could smell her perfume. "Yes?" she said, almost as an affirmative challenge.

"We'll discuss more later, I promise. But I need to ask you absolutely not to approach our staff. As I'm sure you can appreciate, this is going to be a sensitive issue," I said, nodding as if that would make her nod in agreement. "We've worked out a strategy and will share it with you later." I stopped talking and nodded again. "Now, I'm sorry but I really have to keep moving." I was glad to see Doug and Susan coming toward us. "Pineapple upside down muffins in just another few minutes," I said.

"SUPER!" they said back in unison.

Just as I fit the last leaf into the table, our manager Alissa arrived to complete the table setting. I ducked into the kitchen to get the muffins out of the oven just at the stroke of eight. I gently placed them on a platter with a big doily and delivered them as Mrs. Mark was refilling her coffee. "You'll love these muffins," I said to no one in particular in a cheery voice, putting them on the counter and reaching for a stack of small plates.

"I've never been a big fan of pineapple, or muffins, for that matter," she said. I returned to the kitchen, unable to find words to respond.

At the stroke of nine, I returned to the dining room to call people to breakfast. Small crystal bowls of fresh rhubarb sauce greeted the guests. Watching them circle around to their usual spots, I found myself relishing the fact that this was Mrs. Mark's last day. I couldn't help noticing that she was hovering, as if she might *not* be planning to sit down. Then I began to worry that she'd start talking about the disappearance of her necklace.

"Here's a seat here," I said to her husband as he came in, fresh from a walk. "Are you going to join your husband?" I was determined to sound gracious. Since they'd missed the first two breakfasts due to golf, this was their first actual seating. I felt relieved when Mrs. Mark joined her husband and seemed to engage in conversation with a friend sitting on her other side.

Returning to the kitchen, I found an aproned David standing in front of the griddle that straddled two burners of the stove. I love how he looks in his apron when he's being bacon man – moving pieces back and forth, putting the press on top of wrinkly ones. He's become masterful at it.

"What's going on out there?" he asked.

"The dining room's under control," I said, whispering into his ear so he'd hear me even with the vent fan on. "I'm going to go to the office to get all the bills ready. Okay?"

"Yeah. Go ahead. I already briefed Alissa on 'the case.'"

Everyone else had checked out when Mrs. Mark came to the office to pay and once and for all, discuss the missing necklace.

"We have quite a bit to discuss," she said. "I'd planned for this to be a very pleasant stay, but I'm afraid losing my very favorite piece of jewelry has ruined that. I'm mad at myself, because I actually thought to put all my valuables in my pocketbook when we went to play golf. But maybe it was already missing then." She looked up at me with a little smile that I would describe as more vicious than a witch's.

"Not to worry. I'm quite confident we're going to get to the bottom of this. Here is our plan: We will call our insurance agent, and the police if we have to. Of course, we're going to stay in touch with you each step of the way. I wonder if you know its approximate value?" I sounded like a detective on CSI.

She pushed her hair away from her eyes. First one side. Then the other. I learned in a Human Dynamics class once that this was nearly always a sign of uncertainty, a lack of confidence. "I just can't say. Believe me though, it was a lot. *A lot.*"

"In the meantime, let's settle your bill," I said, handing her a copy of it. "I'll be sure to tell the insurance people that and the police, if we have to. Is this what you were expecting to pay?" I asked.

"Honestly, I was hoping you might have a little compassion and offer to reduce our bill. After all, we didn't have breakfast two mornings. That has to equal something. And now the stealing. But you seem to have another way of doing business." She shook her head, and handed me her credit card.

"I'm not sure we operate any kind of special way, Mrs. Mark, but I promise if there does turn out to be an insurance claim, we'll try to incorporate your lodging costs, if they let us," I said.

"Uh-huh, uh-huh. You talk a good game. I sort of hate to admit this, but I always wanted to own a B&B until this experience. I even had my husband on board."

"Really? And what *exactly* was it that changed your mind?" I asked.

"Duh…being *robbed*, naturally. How would you feel?"

"Oh, of course. How silly of me. I can see you're feeling bad. I do want you to have your Departure Package, though." I handed the bag to her, then swiped her card.

"Whatever is *this*?" she asked, holding it up and looking at it as if it were a poisonous specimen.

Departure Packages got started early in our career as a hedge against leftovers. Each bag contains cookies and fruit. The tradition is now formalized – all the items go in a white paper bag, along with napkins. Then we tie it up with maroon-colored yarn, and tuck a sprig of rosemary (for remembrance, as Shakespeare's Ophelia suggests) in the top.

She made a scribble on the receipt, took the bag and turned to go. Then she turned back, shaking her head slightly. "I certainly hope you'll be meeting with your staff as soon as possible so you can get to the bottom of this. It could ruin your business, you know."

"Hmm-hmm." I got up and followed her out the door of the office.

"One more thing," she said, stopping short. "I'm a therapist and you look like you could use a hug. How about it?"

I stopped short, wishing myself invisible, deciding if I could have a bathroom emergency, wanting desperately to know where David had disappeared to. In the nanosecond before I had to do *something*, the front door opened and David and Mr. Mark crowded into the narrow hallway with us. "What are you two up to?" Mr. Mark asked.

Sylvana Mark's previously outstretched arms had fallen to her sides. She looked toward me. "We're just settling up," she said.

"Yup. Squaring our accounts," I said.

David squeezed past her to stand next to me, arm draped over my shoulders.

"Have a safe journey," I said.

"We'll try, but I can tell you my heart's as heavy as lead," she said, turning. Mr. Mark grabbed her hand and led her out.

David came into the office and said, "Let's not call the insurance guy right away. It's bound to turn up, don't you think?"

"I sure hope so," I said. "Wow. I'm feeling whipped and it's only 11:20 a.m."

At noon, I was back in the office Googling museum shops in New Mexico, desperate to determine just how expensive that necklace was. I looked up and there she was, coming down the steps.

"Mrs. Mark! What a surprise to see you again," I said.

She stood at the threshold, shaking her head. "Not as surprised as I was to find your staff in *my* room," she said, leaning toward me with both hands clutching the doorway, her hair encasing her face.

"But you checked out! We thought you were on your way home to Eugene. Someone's checking into 'your' room in a few hours, so we had to get it ready."

"You know as well as I do, Deedie, you had your people looking for the stolen necklace, maybe even planting it somewhere," she said.

"Oh, no, no, you're wrong about that," I said.

"Well then, tell me, why wouldn't you just call the police, that's what I don't understand. We got almost to the end of town and I just couldn't leave. I had to come back. And I told my husband that if the necklace hadn't turned up, we'd just go to the police station ourselves." I came out from behind the desk. "As I told you earlier, Mrs. Mark, I'm sorry you aren't willing to believe us. If you think you need to tell the police, I can't stop you, and I won't." I could feel red blotches breaking out on my chest.

"This whole episode has been just too stressful for words. I have to do *something* about it, since it appears you're not going to," she said, her voice rising in pitch.

"As I said earlier, we're going to stick with the original plan. Insurance company, then the police. And we'll stay in contact with you."

"Well, you just do that, Deedie Runkel. And in the meantime, I'll be at the police station doing what really needs to be done." She nodded her head at me and walked out the front door. I heard the car engine start up in the driveway. Her poor husband, I thought.

My sigh as I watched their cream-colored Lexus SUV head out of town reverberated up the stairs so distinctly that Vieve called down to see if everything was okay.

I headed for the living room and the sofa. Now that the house was empty of guests for a few hours, I needed to do a little relaxing. On my back, my head on a pillow, I called David on my cell. "You won't believe this, but she came back and now she's headed for the police station to make the report she's mad that we won't, or should," I said. He was across the street fixing a sprinkler system quirk.

"I'll be there in a minute."

Alissa arrived in the living room as I was hanging up. "I thought you told me she'd checked out," she said. "I couldn't believe it when she started yelling that I was in *her* room."

"I'm sorry. I didn't see her come in. And now she's on her way to file a police report. She's moved on from Nancy Drew, girl detective, to Sergeant Friday."

"What's up now?" David asked as he walked in.

"What's up is we're about to be visited by the Ashland Police Department, courtesy of Sylvana Mark."

"Oh, God. This story is getting more and more endless," he said, giving me a half hug. "Let me know if the police come."

One hour and then another went by without a call from the police. I checked the Department's online log to see if there were any theft reports. I checked Yelp! and Trip Advisor to see if she'd made an adverse report. I went over her room top to bottom, even though the staff already had. Nope. Finally we both decided there was nothing we could do and fretting wasn't going to help, so we went home for dinner, armed with the Sunday *New York Times*.

We were having a second drink when the phone rang. Sylvana Mark had reached home. "I wanted you to be the first to know I found the neck-lace as I was unpacking. It was in a *very* secret compartment in my suitcase."

"'Guess we won't have to call the police after all," I said, nodding to David across the table.

"Oh that wouldn't have been necessary anyway. I already made a report since you weren't willing to. I guess I should let them know," she said.

"We'll be happy to let them know," I said. "Who took the report?"

"I think I'd like to talk to the detective myself," she said. "I have his business card right here. Sig Terrin is his name. I'll call him."

"Okay. We'll let our staff know. They'll be as relieved as we are, I'm sure. They were so upset," I said.

"You see, this is what I meant about owning a B&B. You have to worry about the staff all the time," she said.

"Actually, we don't worry about the staff all the time, Mrs. Mark. Maybe you would, but we don't -- except when they've been falsely accused."

Pineapple Upside Down Muffins

For the topping:

- 1 can of pineapple chunks or 3 apples, peeled and sliced
- ½ cup dark brown sugar
- 4 T unsalted butter
- ½ cup walnuts or pecans, roasted

For the muffins:

- 2 cups all-purpose flour
- ¾ cup dark brown sugar
- 1 T baking powder
- ½ t cinnamon
- ¼ t salt
- 8 T (1 stick) unsalted butter, melted
- 2 large eggs
- ¾ cup sour cream (or plain Greek yogurt)
- 1 t vanilla

1. Heat oven to 375. Generously grease 12 muffin pans.
2. In large skillet over medium heat, stir together fruit, ½ cup brown sugar, 4 T butter and pinch salt.
3. Cook, stirring occasionally, until the apples are tender, about 15 minutes. Distribute fruit among the muffin cups. Add nuts.
4. To make muffins, whisk dry ingredients together. In a separate bowl, whisk together ½ cup butter, eggs, sour cream or yogurt and vanilla.
5. Fold wet ingredients into dry. Distribute batter evenly to tins. Cook 20-22 minutes until muffins are slightly puffed.
6. Allow muffins to cool slightly before turning over on to warm platter.

Yield: 12 muffins.

Be Wild!

It was only 10:15 in the morning, long before our 3 o'clock check-in time, and there stood Peter in the doorway. Startled, I jumped in my seat.

"I want those blackberry scones you made last time I was here as soon as possible. I've been *impossibly* hungry for them every *minute* since I checked out two years ago," he said. Peter excelled at being imperious and this was a perfect example.

"Hello there, Mr. Peter Lawson. How great to have you back. It's been too long…"

"Thank God I got here before the real heat of the day," he said. I desperately tried to recall when he had been here last. "I'm already sopping wet and need to change into something cooler. It's so good to be back."

"We're so glad," I said, getting up to give him a hug.

Sometimes I'm at a loss to discern the best approach to greet returning guests. If I begin by thrusting out my hand, I often find myself grabbed into a warm embrace. If I do a light hug, I can tell at times that it's not entirely welcome — for either the guest or myself. Today, it was the latter, as my hug revealed that Peter's loose-fitting jacket was indeed damp, even a little odorous. On his lapel was an over-sized button -- maybe six inches across -- that read, "Be Wild!" in large red letters.

"I decided to go for the French look today," he said, taking off a soiled white beret, tugging at his jacket, then his striped T-shirt, then the chartreuse bandana around his neck. "Do you think it works?" he asked, doing a demi-pirouette. "Oh, and by the way, I'm sorry my friend isn't going to be with me, which means I can have that small room, right?" I couldn't help noticing he was nearly bald compared to what I remembered. I hoped it wasn't from cancer.

So much time passes between our guests' visits that sometimes the news isn't good when guests eagerly fill you in as if you were a long-lost family member. Clinical details are rarely, to my embarrassment, withheld. Details like that about Peter trickled into my brain. He'd told me at more length than I would have hoped for about his AIDS scare, which included the fact that he was most assuredly not gay, just ask anyone. Turned out it was a skin cancer, as I recollected.

"Actually, that's great. You *can* have Will's Study," I said. "The guest who was going to be there just called to say she *was* bringing a friend and would need a bigger room." I was relieved to solve what could have been two difficult situations so easily.

"And what about that blackberry scone waiting for me?" he asked, picking up a worn leather duffle bag that wasn't zipped up entirely. What looked like underwear bulged out.

"Not yet. You'll have to wait until market day tomorrow," I said. "I'll get a new flat of wild blackberries. But I know you're a patient man, Peter, so you can wait."

"I'm so glad I remembered to come back here," he said. "Show me where to go, 'cause I forget." The last command came in what I now remembered as Peter's petulant voice, which he reserved for stating his needs.

I slithered past him into the narrow hallway, turning left into the living room and then right to Will's Study. "Here we are! Do you think this will work? It looks like you have two stuffed-full bags," I said.

"This will be more than suitable," Peter said, plopping down on the single bed. "I have been going at such a pace getting ready for this trip and my next one. I'm worn out. The problem is, I *still* have trouble sleeping, no matter how tired I am. I'm really looking forward to getting some rest while I'm here."

"Well, I hope you will be able to rest," I said. "Just concentrate on relaxing and enjoying the plays. They're really great this year." The phone began to ring. "We can talk more later, Peter," I added, then rushed away to answer it.

The next morning, as I moved among the guests offering coffee and scone refills, there was a conversational buzz and it wasn't about *Richard III*.

"I had to tell him at 5:30 this morning that he had Maria Callas playing much too loudly," said Mrs. Sarosin (she preferred that we not use her first name, ever), who was in Mother Mary's room, across the living room from Will's Study.

"I came out," Rosalee, another guest declared, "noticed he was comatose and turned the player off. I don't like opera at all, *especially* 'Carmen,' and *especially* not at 6 a.m."

"So, what play did *you* see last night?" I asked Mrs. Sarosin, trying to shift the focus of the conversation. I couldn't help remembering Peter saying he had been having trouble sleeping, and since he was the only one not at the table, it seemed quite likely it was him they were talking about.

"Well, I have to say it was a little difficult at first, as our fellow guest who likes opera at odd hours ended up right in front of me. He was wearing a jeweled crown and a huge peacock-feather mask! It wasn't easy to see beyond him."

Everyone at the table began talking at once. Peter had been asked by the house staff to remove his crown and mask so others could see, but he had put them back on during intermission as he moved through the lobby, a long bluish-purplish cape flowing, they reported.

Oh my God in heaven, was all I could think. A costume, as if he were one of the acting company. And playing the opera all night. What were we going to do with him? I was furious with myself for not remembering Peter better. Wait 'til David heard this.

"Well, did you all like *Measure for Measure* at yesterday's matinee?" I said. "Weren't those mariachis just perfect?"

"He hummed so loud, it distracted everyone around him," Rosalee said. "And he was wearing a big pin that said, 'Be Wild!'"

"Where did you get this guest, honestly?" Mrs. Sarosin asked.

Where did I get this guest? I didn't really want to engage in this discussion. I definitely hadn't remembered him as being so colorful or prone to public antics, but what could I do? I'd reported his arrival to David at dinner the night before and we'd been so tickled about his Be Wild! button that we'd decided *we* ought to be wearing them. But then again, I didn't want to violate the Innkeeper's Golden Rule of not talking about guests to other guests, tempting as it sometimes is.

"Actually, he's been here before," I said. "He knows the theatre quite well, I believe. Maybe when he joins us it would be good to ask him more about the plays. I think he may even have taught theatre at one time."

"I'm sure he got that crown and mask at the Tudor Guild. I saw him in there yesterday afternoon, buying a lot of things," said Katie, one of our younger guests. The Tudor Guild is the gift shop at the Oregon Shakespeare Festival, and nearly everyone seems to visit it at one point or another. "He walked out with three humongous bags."

"Well, I guess it's all related to his "Be Wild" campaign, whatever that is," Vince said.

While they talked, I slipped into the kitchen to alert David to the current topic of conversation at the table.

"They're all just jealous," he said. "They wish they had the nerve, that's all. But let me try to change the subject."

David opened the door to the dining room and disappeared.

His baritone voice rose above the chatter at the table. "I hear there was a play-within-the-play last night, featuring one of your fellow guests," I heard him say. I imagined his big broad grin accompanying this. I could hear laughter.

Within another few minutes, he was back at his sausage post. "Now they're all trying to remember which play has the play-within-the-play and what it's title is. No more Peter!"

"You're amazing, that's what I think," I said.

A few hours later, Peter's – crown-free – head, poked around the half-closed door of my office, where I'd closeted myself to work on changes to our website.

"Any chance a hungry guest could get breakfast?" he asked. He'd awakened in a state of supreme petulance.

"Peter, it's almost noon!" I said. "You know how things work here. We don't serve lunch. Breakfast is at 9! "

"I know. It was my insomnia. I had a terrible night," he said. "You should be feeling very sympathetic to me. And imagining how hungry I must be."

"We did manage to save you a piece of the Will's Pancake David made. I'm sorry you didn't get it straight out of the oven."

"I hardly slept a wink until early this morning," he said. "Thank God for your collection of opera CDs. Maria Callas finally put me to sleep. I'm afraid some of the other guests might have been a little vexed."

"I'll go heat your breakfast up," I responded, "but you're right, the other guests were more than a little surprised to hear opera at full volume at 5:30 a.m. It's against the rules, Peter."

"Sorr-eeeee," he said, in perfect eleven-year-oldese.

I couldn't tell if he was wearing pajamas or another French fashion get-up. His red-and-white striped pants were wide-legged. A massive white tee-shirt hung almost to his crotch. The "Be Wild!" pin was drooping toward his belly button from the middle of the neckline.

When I came out of the kitchen with a plate of heated-up leftovers, he'd already sat down at the head of the table and was adjusting the "Be Wild!" pin.

"This is really a great way to meet people," he said, tapping the button. "Really great."

"Where did you get that? David and I love it," I said, not telling a lie. I returned to the kitchen for his coffee and juice.

"My brother gave it to me for Christmas. I don't know where he got it, but I've been wearing it for months."

"Now, listen. I've got two plays today, so I'm not going to be around much," he said. "I promise to be on time to breakfast tomorrow, though. There seem to be some nice people here. And I need you make me a reservation for dinner tonight at Cucina Biazzi."

"Sure. But you have to show up on time. They're really particular."

"Oh, I will. Don't worry," he said.

We make dinner reservations for guests all the time and I reminded myself I had to treat Peter no differently, even though I couldn't imagine his impact on the small, intimate restaurant just two doors away. After he left, I called Cucina to make the reservation.

"Will there just be one in the party?" Rebecca, the maître'd said.

"Yup, just one. He'll be wearing a big button on his lapel," I said.

"That says what?" Rebecca asked.

"You'll see," I said. "Thanks for making room for him."

It was an "elbows down" breakfast the next morning, with fourteen people squeezed around the table as the last of the June rains fell outside. We call it 'elbows down' when we have to squeeze both chairs and people around the table, leaving no excess room for free range of motion of the elbows. Peter was the last to arrive, wearing a flowing white surplice that could have been a nightshirt, a bright pink kerchief around his neck and a purple golfer's cap with built-in sparkles. Not surprisingly, his accessory pin sat securely near his puffy right shoulder. A very attractive thin young lawyer in running clothes moved her chair closer to her mother's to make space for him.

In the kitchen, I found Camelia and Vieve comparing notes. They both work concessions at the theatre evenings and apparently they'd encountered Peter the night before. They reported that he was ensconced in a flowing royal blue velvet cape, crown and peacock mask. And he apologized for using his credit card to buy the wine because he was a little "cash short." *But*, he'd told them, he'd soon be making a bundle starring in a Japanese porn movie. Camelia admitted to being curious as to what role a six-foot tall bald white man with a paunch would play.

"Listen," I said, smiling at the thought of Peter in the movie. "We have to treat him with the same respect we do all the other guests. It's okay to be amused, but we can't treat him any differently, right?" We all nodded at each other and then had a short giggle.

I picked up the pitchers of juice to make my rounds. "I'll get the flowers for the plates," Vieve said.

"I think we have enough nasturtiums," I said.

Camelia was lining up the plates on the counter.

In the dining room, I found David pouring coffee and passing my vaunted blackberry scones while the guests talked quietly among themselves.

"I'm going to have two of these divine scones," Peter said. "I've waited a long time to have them again. Thanks, Deedie. They're perfect." He tipped his hat at me, then took it off and plopped it on the table in front of him, narrowly missing the flower arrangement.

Turning to the young woman next to him, he asked, "Are you an actor? You're pretty enough to be one." He leaned toward her, winking.

"No, I'm a lawyer in San Francisco," Kate said, pulling away a bit. "I come here for the theatre. You're right about the scones, though. They are perfect."

"How positively fascinating," Peter said. Then, raising his voice, he said, "Would any of you have guessed this little lass is a lawyer?"

Everyone at the table looked away and resumed their own conversations. I'd heard the exchange in the kitchen and stomped my foot on the floor. Everyone looked up from what they were doing, curious about my stomping.

"I'm just hearing Peter make a pass at Kate and proceed to humiliated her. Damn him."

David was busy turning the ham. "Honey," I said to him, "we can't have Peter capitalizing all the guests attention. Aren't you concerned?"

"I think we should get him to talk about his film experience," he said. "Camelia just told me about it." He was smiling the smile I'd fallen in love with more than 40 years earlier. A broad smile with perfect, straight white teeth.

After that endless day, we were both exhausted and went to bed early. Aside from the constant demands of the full house, we'd been awakened by the answering service at 2 a.m. the night before because Peter had lost his key to the front door. "Sleepus interruptus," as we call it, takes its toll on the next day (which it had) and in this instance, our tolerance for which ever guest called.

"He'd better not call tonight," David said. "And I love you."

I heard the phone first, four hours later, at 2:15 a.m. The answering service had Peter on the line again, with the same issue as the night before -- he had the key this time, but couldn't make it work.

"Hey, Peter, I said. You may have to wiggle the key a little once you have it the lock. Do you have it there now? What's the matter? You can't see the lock? You can't see the lock because you have a mask on? Peter, take the mask off. Okay. Let's try again. You've got to be as quiet as possible. All the other guests are asleep. No, I'm not coming to do it for you. You know how to put a key in a lock. Try again, please. Okay. Okay. We are coming. Stay right where you are and please be very, very quiet. Just sit down on the chair. You can't keep doing this. Good night."

By now, David was awake, out of bed and pulling on his sweat pants for the trip up the block to unlock the front door. When he returned, he was as mad as I'd ever seen him as an innkeeper.

"That guy's not just wild, he's a crazy son of a bitch. You should have seen him in that costume and he still had the friggin' mask on. No wonder he couldn't even find the lock. I'm completely done with Peter. We need to be able to *sleep*. I don't mind real emergencies, but this is just stupidity," David said, returning to bed.

"I agree, I agree. But what are we going to do?" I said.

As we went over Peter's stay thus far, we realized he had managed to disturb or offend everyone in the inn, not least of all, ourselves. We couldn't risk losing guests because he was committed to being wild. And even though one couldn't help but be amused by his antics, there was always the chance that it could ultimately damage our reputation.

"He's already done some damage, "David said. "By the time I got there, the Sarosins were up, worried that someone was breaking in. She told him not to dare put any opera on and he went quietly to bed. Which is what we need to do right now. It's way after three."

"Did you try talking to him?" I asked, snuggling.

"Oh, God, no. He'd had way too much to drink. Mrs. Sarosin told him that as he went to bed. Not sure he heard."

"Good night again."

Peter's reservation had two nights to go.

During our quiet Kitchen Karma time the next morning, we spoke in low voices about the "Peter Issue."

"You said you thought of an alternative while you were shaving. What kind of an alternative are you talking about?" I asked David.

"I'm thinking we need to find him a new hotel, like the Stratford. We tell him we just can't accommodate his needs." By now he had put the two different hams – turkey and regular – on to a serving plate and was trying to find the right fork.

I went back to the dining room, carrying three plates. The goal every morning is to get hot plates out as fast as possible, women first, larger servings for men. Everyone went straight to eating and I was relieved that there was no longer any focus on Peter.

When I returned, David said, "I just checked and the Stratford Inn has room for him, but let's wait until after breakfast and I'll have a talk with him."

"I think this is the right decision, much as I hate to admit defeat," I said. "We've had some challenges in the past, but no one has been so dedicated to *being wild*."

"Or in Japanese porn movies," Camelia said.

"Or wearing crowns to the plays," Alissa said.

"Don't forget the peacock mask," David said.

"Deedie, don't forget to call Catherine back. She called while you were in the dining room."

"Okay. David, let me call Catherine and see what she has to report from the theatre before you talk to him," I said.

"Oh, Deedie, you wouldn't have believed it," she reported. "He's quite a sizable man and he wore this huge flowing cape and a crown. Others saw him in a mask. Anyway, when the cast takes its first bow, *he* stands up, turns around and bows a few times to the audience, then turns around again and begins mad waving, bowing and scraping at the cast. The house staff was thinking of calling security, it was so wild. Did you know all this?" Catherine asked.

"We've heard and experienced quite a bit of it. It's safe to say, we're not surprised," I replied. "Thanks, dear friend. We'll talk later."

David caught Peter before he went back to his room.

"Hey, Peter. We need to talk. Can you come in here a minute?" He motioned for Peter to join him in the office. David sat behind the desk, while Peter sat across from him.

"I feel like I might be in the principal's office," Peter said. "I know I've been bad, but that breakfast was sensational." He put his purple cap back on.

"'So glad you liked the breakfast, Peter. That's great. And you haven't been bad, it's just that we've been thinking about your stay here and realize that you seem to need a 24-hour desk to assist you. As you know, we don't have that and it's really hard for us when we have to lose sleep, or our guests do, because of your insomnia or losing your key. I hope you understand. What we've done is find you a new place. What do you think?"

"Oh, God."

"We've checked with the Stratford Inn right behind us and they have a 24-hour desk, and a room for you. I'd be happy to help you take your things over there."

Peter was uncharacteristically quiet for a moment, then perked up.

"You know, David, Mick Jagger's been thrown out of a few hotels, so I guess I'm not in such bad company," he said.

"That's right, you're not," David said, relieved.

I stepped into the office just as Peter was getting up. I wasn't sure what to say. Peter spoke first.

"Any chance I could take some of those blackberry scones you made this morning with me?" he asked. "They were wild and good. I wouldn't mind having the recipe, either."

"Absolutely," I said. "The girls are getting the departure packages together right now. I'll tell them you prefer scones."

One thing I was sure of as I watched David walk Peter toward his new lodging was this -- if he called again, we'd be full.

Fresh Fruit Scones

Preheat oven 450 degrees.

- 1 1/3 C. flour
- 2/3 C. cornmeal
- 2 T. granulated Sugar
- 2 T. packed brown sugar
- 1 ½ t. baking powder
- ¼ t. baking soda
- ½ tsp. salt
- 1/3 C. butter
- I <u>sliver</u> Granny Smith apple

1. Put dry ingredients in food processor and cut up butter and process until mixture resembles course crumbs. Make a well in center.
2. Combine

   - ½ C. buttermilk
   - 1 egg
   - 1 ½ t. finely shredded lime peel

3. Add to flour mixture and stir with a fork.
4. Add 1 C. berries and mix gently.
5. Use a large spoon or scoop to drop the mixture onto a baking sheet.
6. Bake 12 to 15 minutes or until golden brown. Shift trays from top to bottom and turn around halfway through.
7. Icing

Whisk enough lime juice into 1 cup powdered sugar to make into drizzling consistency. Drizzle over warm scones. (*This is a key step. Do not skip in interest of less sugar.*)

Bottom Line Organic

We didn't read lots of books about innkeeping before we welcomed our first guest, but we did solicit advice from everyone we knew. One of the first to offer counsel was our daughter Sara, an organic farmer.

It was simple and direct. She said, "Be totally organic."

This was way back in 2002 when to be organic, one had to spend approximately double on everything on their grocery list.

"You're right, we probably should be," I said. "But we just can't afford to be *totally* organic, at least not yet." When Sara first embraced Organic with a capital "O," we were even less able to afford the tariff organic entailed, so there was slight mother-daughter tension on the subject. While I totally endorsed the notion of being organic, paying twice the price for our Christmas rib roast might leave stockings empty and the rest of our plates bare save for meat, I informed her. Long ago as it was, we both remembered that non-organic hunk of cow that somehow managed to be edible.

"Mom, Dad, you'll see, it will make a difference to your guests," she responded.

"You should at least try."

We said we would.

Not long after that, one of our housekeepers told us about her friend, Jackie. Jackie lives up the road from us and chickens are her hobby. She'd launched her career as a purveyor of unusually good eggs when she realized her six different breeds of chickens laid lots more eggs than she knew what to do with. *Sara will be pleased, I thought.*

"I won't always have all you need," she said in a loud voice in our first phone conversation. "If that's okay, and also if it's okay that I go on vacation sometimes and we have to make other arrangements, okay?" she said. "I'll be there tomorrow."

Her aging, mildly-battered silver truck pulled in the driveway exactly at two the next day. Our new egg lady came up the front steps slowly, a bag with eight cartons each in either hand. "Here they are. Have a look," she said, sitting down wearily. Beads of perspiration ran down her cheeks from blunt pixie-cut grey hair. A large woman, she wore a colorful caftan over matching aqua shorts and had color-coordinated flip flops on her feet. Peacock feather earrings with a touch of the same color dangled from her ears.

"Open up one of them cartons so's you can see what all chickens I have," she said, fishing a carton out of one bag.

I opened it up to find a palette of colors ranging from light brown to grey to pale blue to one nearly as aqua as her shorts. Three of them had the name of the chicken that laid them written in pencil: Emmy, Rose, Mary.

"These are terrific," I exclaimed. "Why do some have names and some don't?"

"I dunno. Guess I had a pencil with me when I picked 'em up." she said matter-of-factly. "And they're pretty much organic, too. Don't know if you care about that, but the fancy restaurant where I deliver does." Then she dug into another bag and brought another carton of much larger, dull white eggs. "These I got from our ducks. These are the best for baking, believe me. You want them too?"

"Sure," I said. "I'll give them a try. They're *huge.*"

Now that she's been our egg provider for nearly 12 years, Jackie lets herself in on Wednesday afternoons and helps herself to whatever scones might be languishing in the cake-saver on the counter. She says it's all for her husband, Wayne, but we've always suspected some sharing goes on. We keep a running tab on the counter, where she writes how many dozen she delivered, and how much we owe or she does, based on the amount of cash we leave out for her. At $3.00 a dozen, we feel we're getting an incredible deal in this valley where $6.00 isn't an unusual price for organic eggs. Inflation has apparently never had an impact on her business.

We have learned to check them before we put them in the 'fridge, though, because sometimes a few feathers peek out from a box, fastened by dry chicken shit. We don't mind their presence, but our health inspector does. We lost five points on our inspection one year because a tiny grey tuft peeked out of a carton.

"You know, the reason your scones are so pretty and yellow is cause of my eggs," she told me one week when I happened to be in the kitchen. "Their yolks are more golden. Especially those leghorns. Or, it could be the duck eggs." She stopped for a moment to mull this over.

Sara was delighted when I told her Jackie had become one of our vendors. When I told her how much we were paying, she said, "Mom, that's not nearly enough! You should pay her more."

"We're paying her what she charges, honey. It's a good deal. We thought you'd be glad to hear they're organic."

"I am, but I can't see how Jackie's making any money," Sara said. "Maybe you should check on others when the Farmer's Market starts."

"I guess we have to be more concerned about our bottom line than Jackie's," I said back.

When Jackie had to have surgery on her bum knee, our egg arrangement nearly came to a halt. We worried we wouldn't be able to find as good or reliable a supplier. Then Jackie called with a solution.

"My neighbor's gonna help us out while I'm in the hospital. But she can't deliver cause she's a teller at the Bank of the Cascades. So what would you think about pulling into the drive-in window on Wednesdays and she'll have them for you. That gonna work?"

"Well, sure, sure," I said, thinking David could stop on the way home from his weekly bridge game. "What's your friend's name?"

"I call her Jojobean, have since we were in the tenth grade together. But I think you all maybe ought to call her Joyce. Okay?"

Returning from the first week's drive-in pick-up, David was delighted and amazed that bank personnel hadn't blinked when he said he was there to pick up eggs.

"Makes you wonder what else we might be able to pick up there," he said.

Before long, the weekly Farmer's Market opened. I always get excited on the first day every year. Something about Farmers' Markets always makes me feel close to the earth. Wandering from stall to stall, I was dazzled by all the opportunities to be organic. If it wasn't tomato plants and petunias, it was huckleberries and heather. The Armory parking lot, usually filled with camouflaged trucks and a sprinkling of soldiers, oozed with good things to eat and plant. An organic mecca. I couldn't help noticing that everything cost considerably more than nearly everywhere else we shopped. I felt a pang of guilt for having these thoughts, knowing Sara would think it was fair value. Any reluctance I had to spend more for organic receded totally when I saw all the flats of delectable organic berries.

"Okay if I test a few?" I asked Cathy Pennington.

"Sure, sure," she said, smiling, almost daring me not to buy them.

I had to stop myself before I ate an entire basket of the red raspberries. The blues were bigger than I'd ever seen. Sheepishly, I took half a handful. I looked up to see Cathy nodding my way.

"Pretty good, huh?" she said.

"I have a B&B," I said. "These are for our guests."

"I can give you a break if you buy a flat," she offered.

Trying to navigate back to my car dodging the swarms of people at market while balancing four flats of fresh blueberries, red and yellow raspberries and strawberries, I nearly ran into a fellow innkeeper. "What are you going to do with all those berries? Make jam? How will you have time to do *that?*"

"Oh no," I assured her. "These are for the guests. They'll love them and they're so fresh. Don't you get them too?"

"Of course we serve berries this time of year. But I'd *never* buy them here. They're *so* much cheaper at COSTCO, and just as good."

"Hmm. You're right about the cost," I said. "But I'm not totally convinced about the taste."

When I got home, I sheepishly reported my encounter to David and revealed just how much they cost.

"How about we let the guests decide what's best for them?" David suggested. "I'll get some at COSTCO and we'll put them to a comparison test with Pennington's tomorrow. What do you think?"

"Sounds like a great idea," I said, " But are we prepared to continue serving the more expensive alternative if that's what they vote for?"

"I think it's basically a bottom line question," David, the chief financial officer of our operation stated flatly.

"So you mean if the guests decide Pennington's berries are better, we'll keep getting them and just won't make as much money, right?" I asked.

"Right," David said. "But the guests will want to come back and tell their friends about us if they like what they're fed, so ultimately it *will* be good for the bottom line. Sara's prediction that consumer demand for organic is growing seems to be proving correct."

"Got it," I said.

The great Better Berry Tasting occurred the next morning during the fruit course. Each plate had a hefty handful of mixed berries from COSTCO on the right and the same array from Pennington's on the left. I explained the assignment to the guests, trying to sound as unbiased as possible. They were eager to dig into a plate fit for a *Gourmet* magazine cover.

"You have a job today. We're trying to decide where to buy our berries, based on your opinion. We're asking you to be our official tasters," I said. Tell us which side is most pleasing to your palate. Taste. Looks. Texture. You evaluate your experience." As I talked, I gave each guest a tiny ballot on a post-it and a pencil.

Anne Hathaway's Better Berry Tasting	LEFT	RIGHT
Blueberry taste		
Blueberry size		
Blueberry texture		
Raspberry taste		
Raspberry size		
Raspberry texture		

"All you have to do is mark 'left' or 'right'. If you think there's no difference, I guess you can mark both."

An air of enthusiasm reigned as the guests picked up their forks. I ducked back into the kitchen to work on the main course.

About ten minutes later, I sent the staff out to collect the berry plates and ballots. They returned with mostly empty plates, though a few had left some of the berries on the right from Costco. Did they not finish them because they weren't any good, I wondered.

Thankfully, there were no reports of voter fraud, donor fraud, undue influence, hanging chads or money laundering during the balloting. As the self-appointed ballot counter, it didn't take me long to determine the Best Berry. Still holding the ballots in my hand, I went outside to announce the results.

"Pennington Berries are the winners! It was unanimous," I said excitedly. Before I had a chance to say anything else, guests began offering more opinions.

"The ones on the right were watery and tasteless," Mary Turner said, throwing her head back and laughing. "I didn't even finish mine."

"Not only that, they were gritty," Tod Goldberg said authoritatively, looking around and nodding his salt and pepper head to see if everyone didn't agree with him. "That wasn't a very hard vote, Deedie. What's our next test?"

"We'll have to see," I said. "This is our first public poll."

I could hardly wait to get to market the next week to inform Cathy Pennington of her runaway rout at the Hathaway polls.

When the Turners checked out the next day, they said how much they appreciated our commitment to local and organic.

"We know it's more spendy to get those local berries," Paul said, using a synonym for expensive that I hadn't heard before moving to Oregon, "But I think you're going to find it worthwhile to go organic. You should put it on your website."

"What a great idea," I said. "We will. And if you have a moment, you can tell Trip Advisor," I said. We had recently been convinced by our kids that suggesting this to loyal guests couldn't hurt, especially if we wanted to attract a younger, greener group.

"I have another idea," Mary broke in. "I always buy some soap and lotion from Emz Blendz when I'm here. She's a teacher-turned-entrepreneur and I just love her stuff. Maybe you should test her products -- I think she's all organic -- against what you're using now and see how they come out."

"Hmm. Good idea," I said. "We've been thinking all those little bottles and soaps that only get used a little are wasteful, even if they are organic."

I shared the suggestion with Alissa, our manager who was also a graduate student in business management and sustainability. The berry project had gotten us all thinking there were more changes we could make that would make us more organic and sustainable. I told her I had an idea for her semester project. "What if Anne Hathaway's became your project?" I asked. "You could evaluate *everything* we do around here for its sustainability, the same way we did with the berries today!"

"Sounds good," she said. "Let me check with my professor. He'll have to approve of the idea."

Anne Hathaway's launched its first Sustainability Study during the first week of October 2009. Alissa put together a grid of every product we used or activity we performed in the interest of each guest's stay in each different room, from beginning to end. Was it energy efficient? Where did it come from? Were there harsh chemicals involved? Could it be recycled? Was it organic? Whether it was the laundry, the kitchen or the shower stall, we asked questions about how it worked and where it came from. New equations emerged, such as calculating the fossil fuel necessary to get our shampoo from North Carolina to Oregon.

Alissa compiled the final report by the end of our season and her semester. The night before she was going to present the final findings, I was a little nervous.

"It feels like we could be on some sort of slippery slope here," I told David.

"How's that?" he asked.

"I mean, if we really want to be sustainable, I suspect we're going to discover we need to change the way we do lots of things and it could get expensive," I said. "I already called Emz Blendz and I know they're going to be more expensive than the ones from North Carolina we've been using.

But we'll eliminate waste because we're going to buy in bulk and re-use all the same containers!"

"We just have to keep our minds open and be creative," he said. "It could end up being good for our bottom line, just like Sara keeps saying."

"Right, right. The bottom line," I said. "Sometimes I do forget it."

Alissa's Sustainability Study showed there were indeed lots of things we could do, large and small, to reduce our carbon footprint, increase our sustainability, be more organic and stay local.

"We're a little worried about how much it's all going to cost," I said.

"Go to page seven of the document," she said with a professional air. "I've laid out how we can phase in the changes, what the cost will be *and* what the savings will be. Have a look. I bet you're going to be surprised. My professor was, and he should've known."

The table showed there were indeed all kinds of things we could do to become more sustainable -- from removing individual coffeemakers from each room to buying all our soaps and coffee in bulk to being a shareholder in a local organic farmer who would bring us a big box of produce every week -- and help the bottom line at the same time.

"We're talking about a real boost for Anne Hathaway's bottom line," Alissa said. "We're building sustainability in the world, for our vendors and for our guests. Everyone's a winner. And I know it's going to help with the younger guests who tend to look for who's greener. This is going to be a real marketing tool, I'm convinced."

So were we.

"I told you so," Sara said when we called to update her on our Organic Progress.

Irma's Eggs with Organic Eggs

1. Make a cheese sauce: Melt 2T butter and add 2T flour.
2. Add 2 cups of warm milk and when close to boiling add 8 ounces of really good cheddar cheese. Set aside.
3. Sauté onions and peppers in skillet.
4. Scramble a dozen eggs to three-quarters done. Add eggs to cheese sauce and refrigerate overnight.

In the morning, put eggs-cheese mixture into a dish, add sliced mushrooms, top with paprika, bread crumbs and drizzle some melted butter on top.

Bake 35 to 45 minutes at 325

X-Rated Scone Zone

We had great sex.
— Chamomile, 9/14/08

Scones and orgasms aren't often put in the same category. But when I assume my position in the scone zone of our inn each morning, I know the result of my effort is going to produce delight for me *nearly* as satisfying and good.

I begin my meditation there by spreading my legs, squaring my feet, silencing my mind, tuning out the vicissitudes of kitchenry going on about me. I ask myself, "Are you prepared for this quest?" No one hears my answer: "Yes!"

The atmospherics couldn't be more important. A very hot oven. Very hot. Pastry flour's a must, low as it is in protein, producing just the right texture and feel. The slightest hint of sugar reminds us how sweet this enterprise is. Heaping spoons of baking powder ensure what's down will soon rise up. Now to bring them together, key ingredients each with its own special role to play in this act.

I never tire of the essential foreplay – lining up the right tools: a hard plastic spatula, with which to beat the ingredients into submission; a tantalizing soft brush to cool them with cream just before things really heat up; a tiny whisk to convince the cream and eggs this will be a friendly, lasting relationship. And butter – oh, so much butter – to keep things moist. Fresh from the freezer, the butter is reduced to small pieces of lubricating matter with a good-sized knife.

The process moves to the next stage, where different flavors must be introduced. In the past these same guests have favored spicy crystallized ginger, but then to my surprise declared the currants puffed with tawny, well-aged port overwhelmingly the best. The single man staying in Will's Study has expressed a secret desire for amply-sized apricots. How ever can I accommodate everyone when I am just one woman? This thought is never far from my mind.

The glass bowl is best, for it responds readily when moved, unlike the plastic ones with rubber on the bottom. After dumping the ingredients into the bowl, and satisfying myself the necessary chemistry is present, I begin. I make a hole in the middle and gently build up the sides around it with my spatula. These powdery actors have no idea of what will become of them once the waiting cream first seeps, then sweeps its way into my well. To break in now with conversation would ruin the ambiance of the moment, my daily anticipation.

Silently resolute, I fill that hole with the egg-cream combination, the final step toward making all that was separate, one. The ultimate goal, the point of no return – lifting my arm up high, I rejoice as I begin the cutting dance, my left hand wielding the spatula, my right hand spinning the bowl. Fast at first, then slowing as my ingredients wad themselves up into one solid ball. Not yet satisfied, I continue to cut and spin, my muscles aching from the effort, I rise up on my toes to get more leverage.

Ah, now all is moist and ready, a ball, a log, a lump – everyday a different shape, each experience entirely different than the last. My head swirls now with anticipation – I know success is within reach if I am careful, patient, particular. I visualize my guests, counting once more how many are on hand for this particular production. Some are here for the first time, this daily routine unknown to them. I can hear others just beyond the door, getting their coffee, wondering out loud. "Oh, I wish it could be apricot," the wife says to the husband.

I am still counting as I listen. That woman doesn't even know she and the new gentleman have apricots in common. I'll have to tell them. Sixteen, ah, sixteen is easy. My large hands, bones and veins quite prominent, shape the log, smoothing it, lengthening it to its best size, squeezing the creases until they're smooth. Caressing them once they are. One log is sliced in two and then two again. Lumps now, four of them.

How incredible, that sheer minutes ago we had a bowl of just so much flour and now we have four smug little masses, pristine and perfect. Still not sure of their ultimate identity, but clearly aware and ready to achieve their maximum potential. Their ever-loving and creative partner, I, begin. Setting the first one on the shiny granite of my worksite, I pat it down, firmly. I want it to be a perfect circle, which takes some coaching and manipulation from my seasoned fingers, a pinch here, a pat there. The circle smiles back at me, as I put my hands around it for one last shaping. Now is when precision is vital. Now is when a scone becomes a scone. The knife, please, I say to my left hand. And before I know it, I've cut that circle into quarters.

Sliding the slippery steel underneath the emerging morning morsels, I line them up in rows of three across my pan. How wonderfully that French silicone mat protects their bottoms from the heat they'll soon endure – a French kiss with unforgettable impact.

Another circle, another set. Soon we have our sixteen, a perfect platoon, each soon ready to be relished by the guests waiting patiently behind the kitchen door. One last step remains. I take my gentle brush and spread their tops with thick cream, the better to dazzle the taste buds. I turn on my right foot, reach over with my left hand and soon I am walking toward the oven – the march of the scones. If I weren't deep into my meditation, perhaps I would sing with joy, somewhat smug at my accomplishment.

Six minutes and ticking. I prepare the jam pots, knowing they always enhance and heighten desire. Rhubarb and apricot are the chosen ones today. How will they go down? I am always wondering at this stage, wondering who will want what when they put their treasured scone upon their plate.

The timer signals time for an adjustment of the pans. Donning my hot mits, I turn each tray around and reverse their positions on the shelves. Perfection is what I seek and I acknowledge that. Each scone must have the perfect glaze, an even tan, and this I've learned is the best way to accomplish that. Six more minutes now and time to prepare the vessel for these precious products of my making. I remain quiet still, even as I reach for the basket, the napkin and the doily. The burden of my responsibility is great, but feels light after all these years and thousands of scones. I am determined that all who behold what we have come together to create will also appreciate this journey of mine with a heightened consciousness of its inherent beauty…and its taste sensation. This is a powerful feeling I have – what my hands have created will now be treasured by others as it is consumed.

"The scone bell went off." My husband David interrupts my reverie as I am writing the day's menu down for all to see.

"Do they look good enough to eat?" I ask, as always, knowing the answer before I finish speaking.

I lift each one gingerly and place it in the basket carefully. Arranging these gems correctly is the final step before they leave my custody, destined for the mouths of others. With the hypotenuse facing the wall of the basket, first one and then the rest go round on the first level, and then the second. Look at them all, gathered there.

"Is it scone-thirty yet?" a guest asks from the doorway.

"We're just about ready. Coming right now," I say, folding the napkin over them carefully, first the sides and then the tops joining to form a diamond. "They're apricot today."

Thus comes the climax of my daily drama in the scone zone.

JaneAnne's Buttermilk syrup

- 1 cup butter
- 2 cups buttermilk
- 2 cups sugar
- ¼ cup light corn syrup
- 1 t baking soda
- 2 t vanilla

1. Combine the first five ingredients in a pot with high sides.
2. Bring to a boil and let it boil for 7 minutes or so, constantly stirring, until it gets to a nice amber color. It will froth up.
3. Add the vanilla when it cools.
4. This syrup can be kept in the fridge for several weeks.

N.B. Since you already have the essential scone recipes, I've included above another key recipe that others have declared orgiastic in nature and impact. I regularly tell guests it has crack cocaine in it, but you will notice that it is not listed as an ingredient. This goes well with Huckleberry Babies, Auntie Netts' French Toast and other recipes one regularly serves with maple syrup. JaneAnne insisted on making it on her first visit to us near the outset of our career, much to the delight of nearly a zillion guests since.

Departure Package

Our revels now are ended. These our actors,
As I foretold you, were all spirits and
Are melted into air, into thin air:
And, like the baseless fabric of this vision,
The cloud-capp'd towers, the gorgeous palaces,
The solemn temples, the great globe itself,
Yea, all which it inherit, shall dissolve
And, like this insubstantial pageant faded,
Leave not a rack behind. We are such stuff
As dreams are made on, and our little life
Is rounded with a sleep.

William Shakespeare
From The Tempest, Act 4 Scene 1

It's been three years since we buried St. Joseph. As with most things we've undertaken as innkeepers, coming to the decision to sell emerged slowly over the course of several months. We were tired. I'd been a little sick. We were more than 70. Other people were selling and the market showed signs of a rebound from a downswing. And even though we never mean to **retire**, *retire* we were and are still ready to do something else besides work our heads off everyday. Or answer the occasional desperate phone call at night about how to operate the air conditioning. Or remind staff that dead

231

flowers weren't pleasing to guests, nor are rooms without towels. Or windows with streaks and cobwebs. And more than one ant. To mention a few.

We also couldn't help noticing that we'd exceeded the average number of years (seven) most innkeepers last by more than a third.

One of the hardest things after admitting we were tired, which was something we'd only done about three times in our lives, was telling guests. But that's how we found out about St. Joseph and how he could perhaps help us. Asking for help, by the way, is another thing we're not good at. But our guest Jane Ginsburg, a lawyer, has great credibility and she assured us St. Joseph would work for us even though we were saintless Quakers borne of saintless Presbyterians.

Imagine my surprise when all I had to do was Google "St. Joseph home sales" to get over 1,022 hits and opportunities to purchase everything from your basic plastic statue to the deluxe kind suitable for the mantelpiece, which is where one should move St. Joseph once the sale is accomplished and his work is done.

Our first saint statue arrived in good order and the same day, cloudy with rain wanting to fall, we took first one and then the other plastic image out for burial in the front gardens of the Inn and Garden Suites. David dug what he thought was a proper hole for a saint five inches tall.

"Make it deeper," I said. "It says the deeper he is, the more eager he will be to get out." The instructions said this, for true.

"Deedie! You're taking this way too seriously," David said.

"We have to <u>believe</u>. You have to <u>believe</u>," I said. The instructions said it wasn't unusual for there to be a certain amount of levity and disbelief around this ritual, but also that a little solemnity would enhance the effect. I took this to mean I should sing the "Gloria patria," which I did in Sunday school. To my surprise, David remembered the words also.

At this moment in Spring of 2017, St. Joseph seems satisfied to remain under a large patch of lovely lavender heather on one side of the street and orange calendula on the other. He shows no sign of budging, or wanting to be rescued. No buyers have emerged to relieve us of our duties so we can begin our next chapter. In the meantime, we've passed 75, I've had serious health issues and the landscape of the hospitality business has changed dramatically.

I would be the first to suggest that strategies are not our long suit (though David may take umbrage with this). We've never necessarily had a financial strategy nor have we consciously had a strategy for life fulfillment. It's all just happened in an organic way, whatever that implies. Lately, I like to think that when we make our final exit, our life story might be referred to as the Runkel Paradigm, at least by our children.

Anyway, each year the inn's been on the market, we've experimented with methods of "stepping back." We hired a manager who would both manage and cook and discovered our personalities weren't a good match. Then we realized it was silly to try to replace the two of us high-energy, high-achievers, with one person whose energy level was normal. We tried having two people -- a manager and a cook. This was a perfect solution except for two major problems: Cook not showing up and Cook forgetting to put flour in cake (more than once). Despair became our constant companion, along with the chaos that ensues when there either isn't a cook or the cook can't cook and serves inedible food. Our son, Marshall, did come up with a solution to the cook not showing up one weekend when he was on duty -- he took the guests out to breakfast! We applauded his creativity, but we all agreed it wasn't a sustainable practice.

Analyzing why it was so difficult to find and train people to carry on for us became our focus. In a way, it was like learning the business the first time around. But now we had to take an unvarnished look at what we'd created and what goes into making it a success and then try to figure out how to train others to do what we did. This has been the most daunting effort we've ever undertaken, somehow.

Details. Details. Details, like dusting tops *and bottoms* of furniture, polishing the silver, keeping the sugar bowls filled and lights on in the evening -- those were all important things to us that others couldn't seem to accept were essential. But more than that was getting the correct names on the welcome blackboards in each room, having the right, matching china in each Garden Suite, taking clothes left behind out of drawers before the next guest opened them up. We kept being aghast that these things were being missed and porches weren't swept either!

Ownership. We decided it was our keen sense of ownership -- of both the inn and the guest experience -- that fueled our joint obsessive compulsive disorder when it came to details. Not to mention the keen sense of stewardship we feel toward all the family furniture, art and antiques. *This* is what we'd failed to equip our staff with. We couldn't expect them to have it if we couldn't somehow imbue them with the same sense of mission and purpose that had driven us for so many years.

But even if we managed to, we couldn't imagine it would leave the Kitchen Aide and Cuisinart impervious to being broken. We'd never broken them, but now they were broken. What was going wrong?

We felt like we'd run out of strategies, energy, patience and luck. Whatever was St. Joseph doing down there? I considered digging him up so I could tell him directly we needed more attention, and then replace him with the more deluxe model the cheapskate in me had passed up. Our realtor, a B&B owner himself, said there just weren't many lookers these days, alas. He's not a big believer in you-know-who.

Friends have grown weary of hearing how weary we are. Many have offered counsel that reinforced the notion that our business has changed so dramatically that maybe there isn't as much of a market for B&Bs because there aren't as many people who want to stay in one. Our good friend Lynn gave us something she'd inadvertently purchased at a silent auction -- a consultation with a 'business transition' expert. No one could be more ready than we were for a transition. We made an appointment immediately.

By now we'd decided our goal ought to be to make our properties seem more attractive to investors. We'd heard from some of our few potential buyers their fears about how labor intensive the business was and how they were unprepared to work 24/7.

Our consultant's adding machine whizzed through a possible profit and loss sheet for a new business model that leaned more toward the very low maintenance AirBnB approach. Guests let themselves in. Coffeemakers in their rooms. Our heads whirred at the thought of not being on call, the thought of which makes us lose sleep even if there are no calls. Or having to hire someone to be perky in the morning. Or returning to scone duty when the cook doesn't show up.

We spent the rest of the week concentrating on how to reduce the total under the Loss column. It was during that week of cooking up new ideas that David emerged with the notion that if we eliminated breakfast altogether, we could save a bunch of money and untold management hassles. Undeniably, guests love gathering around our tables every morning, but fewer and fewer of them seem to relish the 1,772-calorie breakfast. More than a handful require gluten-free offerings. Another cohort want plain eggs or oatmeal (steel-cut only). And the more variety that got delivered to the table, the more demand developed. Maybe we were just trying to justify one of the most difficult business decisions we've made, but we concluded that breakfast had crossed the threshold into unsustainability -- financially, foodwise and personnel-wise. We sent the following letter to everyone who already had a reservation:

Dear Friends:

After much soulful consideration, we've reluctantly decided that after 15 years of running the inn as a typical bed and breakfast, we no longer can continue as we have in the past and need to adopt a new operational system for the upcoming season....

First and foremost, we've decided to close the kitchen. Coffee and a pastry will be provided, however, for all Inn guests....

This comes with our hopes that you'll understand and know how much we value your ffriendship and loyalty.

We of course worried that people would cancel and send us written brickbats excoriating us for destroying the legend of Anne Hathaway as they'd come to know it. Bad dreams where our Inboxes overflowed and became an anti-Runkel running ticker tape on the front of the Inn, with townspeople gathered outside to cheer, infected our sleep. Thankfully, our inboxes did overflow, mostly with messages that made us read them and weep. An outpouring of support and understanding so overwhelming that we couldn't help but believe we would survive.

Judging from the fact that there were over 30 B&Bs in town when we arrived and there are now less than half that, our business as we knew it is definitely on the wane. Ashland-bound guests are now just as likely to head to Yelp, Google and Trip Advisor as they are to the VRBO or AirB&B websites, or Expedia or any one of dozens of others. Hospitality destinations have become beholden to the latest search engine. Everyone seems to have their oars in the water. We take bookings from all of them and very rarely have any contact with new guests before they arrive. It used to be we'd at least know the names of their grandchildren before they crossed the threshold, just from chatting on the phone.

Our future is now in the hands of St. Joseph, our realtor Graham, our business transition expert Linda, our gifted as well as countless friends and relatives. Ooops. I forgot to say the Universe. While the joy of innkeeping may very well have diminished some for us these last years, we cherish all that it brought us. The experiences recounted herein are but a few of unaccounted daily adventures bursting and bubbling with fun.

Too bad I wasn't able to squeeze in the part about the truck running into one of our rooms -- the only one with a glass-enclosed porch, on which a guest was thankfully not relaxing. The driver had a front seat full of computer air cleaner, which apparently isn't a good thing to sniff when you're driving. This made us glad we were well insured.

Or how we changed the paint inside the rooms from boring white to a veritable panoply of color, leading people to praise the change and ask who our color consultant was. This built our confidence no end.

Molly Ivins would have written her own chapter if she'd lived to tell the story of sitting around here one night drinking scotch, telling about the Texas legislator who hired his brother-in-law to shoot him in the arm so he'd at least get a sympathy vote, not having done another solitary thing during his term. Fortunately, the legislature was nimble enough to pass legislation against doing just that and the guy was arrested. This is one of our most delicious recollections.

We ask guests in the maroon book of knowledge to please let us know should they have to call 911. A pair of sisters called to tell us they'd noticed one of the pesky deer in the back yard was limping, so they gave the dispatcher a ring, brimming as they were with sympathy. "We'll send someone out to shoot her if you'd like us to," was the response. The guest reported immediately that the doe had just had a remarkable recovery. No need to come. This taught us there are alternatives to deer eating all your flowers if you call 911.

Few innkeepers can claim that a guest has saved their life. We unabashedly give credit for that to Dr. Steven Fugaro, whom we consulted by email when I was critically ill in April 2016 in the hospital here. Working with my primary care physician Steven Hersch, he managed to get me airlifted to UCSF Hospital, where I remained for several weeks while the experts fixed my ailing heart. This taught us it's a good thing to ask guests for help when your life depends on it.

Indeed, our departure package bursts forth, bittersweet and loving all at once. Hear, hear to all who made it so!

Rita Feinberg's Coffee Cake

May our dear friend Rita rest in sweetest peace.
At least a million of our guests have swooned over this cake!

- 2 sticks sweet butter
- 2 3/4 C. sugar
- 2 eggs beaten
- 2 C. unbleached all purpose flour
- 1 t. baking powder
- ¼ tsp. Salt
- 1 C. sour cream
- 1 t. vanilla
- 2 C. shelled pecans, chopped
- 1 t. cinnamon

Preheat oven to 350.

1. Cream together butter and 2 C. of the sugar. Add eggs, blending well, then sour cream and vanilla.
2. Sift together flour, baking powder and salt.
3. Fold dry ingredients into creamed mixture and beat until just blended. DO NOT overbeat.
4. In separate bowl, mix remaining ¾ C. sugar w/ pecans and cinnamon.
5. Pour half of batter into bundt pan.* Sprinkle w/ half of pecan-sugar mix. Add remaining batter and top with rest of mixture.
6. Set on middle rack of oven and bake about 1 hour. 10 portions.

Worth timing to be served warm.

*Owning a B&B is a great excuse for buying cool bundt pans. We have one that's a rose and another a sunflower. They've given good service all these years.

EPILOGUE

<hr/>

Peover were eager to dig. We marked off the place of the original burial and offered a free night to the first person to deliver St. Joseph to daylight. One after another of the guests at our Transition Party put down their wine and cake and had a go at it with the ceremonial shovel. Everyone agreed with us that it was important to give credit where it was due. In fact, according to the instructions, he was supposed to be placed reverently on a mantelpiece, once uncovered.

By the end of the afternoon, a deep ditch had been dug in what I had been certain was the exact spot where Joe originally went down. The mystery of what really happened to him will be added to the lore of the Garden Suites, now known as Carlisle Garden Suites. It could be that he is a peripatetic saint and gave up trying to influence potential buyers. (But I do think plastic, like Tupperware, will be one of the relics of our Time on Earth.)

The new owners, Linda Reppond and Walter Carlisle, have bounded on to the scene with the endless energy and enthusiasm we happen to know is essential for success.

We have started writing our new chapter, which will involve promoting this very book as we make our way across the country beginning in June. We want to keep on talking about Scones, even if I'm not making them everyday. Maybe we'll come to your town. Let us know if you're interested: deedie@sconebyscone.com or via our website, www.sconebyscone.com.

If there were space to thank all the people to be thanked, this book would turn into *Scones Karamozov* in no time at all. You know who you are, dear friends, guests and staff. Thank you once again.

About Deedie Runkel

Afer a lifetime on the East Coast of building communities, Donnan Beeson (Deedie) Runkel moved West with her husband David in 2002 to take over a struggling bed and breakfast that caters to theater lovers attending the Oregon Shakespeare Festival. As a friend said, she went from public service to serving the public.

Over many years spent in Baltimore, Harrisburg, Philadelphia, and Washington, Deedie opened a camp for inner-city kids including her own, employed Saul Alinsky tactics to improve lives in an increasing racially segregated city, promoted public libraries and legal aid for older people, and worked to reduce world conflict through the US Peace Corps and the anti-nuclear war organization Peace Links.

Woven throughout these varied endeavors was Deedie's gift for story-telling and writing. She comes from a family of readers and activists whose American roots go back to Quakers who settled in Pennsylvania at the time of William Penn. Her father was both a local politician and the author of an unpublished book on the Molly McGuires, 19th-Century women activists who fought for better conditions for Pennsylvania coal miners.

Deedie majored in English at Penn State, where she met her husband when they both wrote for The Daily Collegian. Just recently, she earned her Master's degree in Fine Arts in writing from UC/Riverside. Her first book, an autobiography titled "Boxes: Lifting the Lid on an American Life" was published in 2010. Her opinion pieces and articles have appeared in The Philadelphia Bulletin, The Washington Post, The New York Times, Friends Journal, and other publications.

She's the mother of three and grandmother of two grandgirls.